Sales by the Book!

Biblical Suggestions for the Sales Professional

TIM CARROLL

ISBN 979-8-89345-526-7 (paperback)
ISBN 979-8-89345-527-4 (hardcover)
ISBN 979-8-89345-528-1 (digital)

Copyright © 2024 by Tim Carroll

All rights reserved. No part of this publication may be reproduced, distributed, or transmitted in any form or by any means, including photocopying, recording, or other electronic or mechanical methods without the prior written permission of the publisher. For permission requests, solicit the publisher via the address below.

Christian Faith Publishing
832 Park Avenue
Meadville, PA 16335
www.christianfaithpublishing.com

Printed in the United States of America

CONTENTS

Introduction vii
Sales Is a Noble Profession 1
Anxious and Worried 3
Make God a Part of Everything We Do 5
Shipwrecked 7
Smile More 9
Be Diverse 11
Hard Work 13
This I Know 15
Don't Cut Corners 17
Exceed Your Customers Expectations 19
Four Anchors of Sales: Persistence (Steadfastness),
Patience, Integrity, and Attitude 21
Persistence 23
Patience 25
Integrity 27
Attitude 29
Walk in Integrity 31
Gain the Whole World! 33
Let Your Yes Be Yes 35
Grumbling 37
Harsh Words 39
Praise 41
Give Me That Mountain 42
Dust Off Your Feet 44
Abide in Me 46
Sing Praise 48
Ask, Seek, and Knock 50
Collaboration 52
Look at the Heart 54
Shrewd as a Serpent 56
Hope Is a Strategy 58

Spiritual Markers	60
Run the Race	62
Humility	64
Quick to Listen	66
Do Not Be Dismayed	68
Preparation	70
Profitable for Teaching	72
Knowledge	74
Ask for Wisdom	76
Reason for Our Hope	78
Fear Not	80
Embrace the Pause	82
Speak with Kindness	84
Simple Obedience	86
Keys to Happiness	88
Physical Movement	90
State of Gratitude	92
For Me, Not to Me	94
Pray Without Ceasing	96
Random Acts of Kindness	98
What Went Well Today	100
Brevity of Life	102
Laughter Is Good Medicine	104
Kudzu Vine	106
Awkward Moments	108
Think before You Speak	110
In the Whisper	112
Have a Plan	114
God, I Can't Hear You	116
Seek His Voice	118
Be Still and Know	120
Recognize His Voice	122
Maintain a Humble Heart	124
Believe and Trust That God Wants to Speak to You	126
God Loves You	128
Keep Pursuing	130

Be Quick to Apologize	132
Fresh Wind, Fresh Fire	134
Get Out of the Boat!	136
Embrace Mondays	138
Failure Doesn't Disqualify You	140
Refresh the Heart	142
Don't Give Up	144
Your War Cry	146
Purpose in Your Heart	148
Pray Fervently	150
Seize the Day	152
Supply Chain Issues and Feeding the Multitude	154
Supply and Demand	156
Vision Statement	157
Give Me Success	159
Be a Person of Valor	161
All Scripture Is God-Breathed	163
Listen before Speaking!	165
A New Thing	167
Count It All Joy	169
Don't Let Bitterness Take Root	171
Reap What You Sow	173
Positive Growth Mindset	175
Use Your Resources	177
Compassion Is Contagious	179
Ask, Seek, and Knock	181
Persevere through the Trials	183
Dead Bones Can Come Back to Life	185
Make A Memorial	187
Power of a Story	189
Ask More Questions	191
When We Are Weak, He Is Strong	193
Finish Strong	195
God Directs Our Path	197
Selfish Ambition	199
Let It Rain	201

Don't Give Up	203
God's Provisions	205
Reason for Our Hope	207
Work Heartily	209
Mustard-Seed Faith	211
Go!	213
To Entertain or Not	215
Never Stop Learning	217
Gratitude Is Contagious	219

INTRODUCTION

If the Bible was given to us for all aspect of our life, it applies to our roles in sales as well. Within the pages of the Bible, there are directions for every decision of life that we may face and must make. It's a learner's guide on how to live our lives. I have spent a large majority of my life in sales and sales management. I have worked in a variety of sales roles in various markets and industries. I know and understand the journey that sales reps take every day. The ups and downs and highs and lows of being a sales professional. It can be a very rewarding career, and it can be one filled with a lot of emotions.

In writing these devotions, I have tried to be careful to not use a verse out of context. The intent of this devotion book is to suggest to my fellow sales representatives there are truths that can help guide us in our sales roles contained in the scriptures if we will take the time to read it; ask God to speak to us and apply what we see.

Our journey starts with making Jesus Christ your personal Lord and Savior. Jesus loves you and wants the very best for you and your life. We just need to trust Him in all aspects of our lives.

Jesus tells us in Matthew 6:33, "But seek first the kingdom of God and his righteousness, and all these things will be added to you."

If you have never asked Jesus into your life, I invite you to say this prayer right now: Jesus, I come before You and ask You to forgive me of my sins. Thank You for dying on the cross for me and for Your forgiveness. I put my whole trust in You. In Jesus's name I pray.

Romans 10:9 says, "If you confess with your mouth that Jesus is Lord and believe in your heart that God raised him from the dead, you will be saved."

Praise the Lord. You have just made the most important decision of your life. I wish you nothing but the best of success throughout your sales career.

SALES IS A NOBLE PROFESSION

> One who heard us was a woman named Lydia, from the city of Thyatira, a seller of purple goods, who was a worshiper of God. The Lord opened her heart to pay attention to what was said by Paul. And after she was baptized, and her household as well, she urged us, saying, "If you have judged me to be faithful to the Lord, come to my house and stay." And she prevailed upon us.
> —Acts 16:14–15

Often, the terms *sales* or *salesman* have a negative connotation. Many people cringe at the very thought they will have to deal with a salesperson. You may even have a negative opinion or be guilty of placing general stereotypes of various salespeople or roles in different industries as well. No doubt, we have all had a negative experience at some point or another in a sales transaction. *Sales*, in its most simplistic definition, is the exchange of a commodity for money. But sales is so much more than simply exchanging money for a product, good, or service. As a true sales professional, you are assisting a potential buyer in deciding about something. You may be helping someone decide about something of very little value, or it may be a life decision that someone is risking their entire future or life savings to make the purchase. Anytime there is an exchange of hard-earned money and you are providing knowledge to help make a well-informed decision, you are performing a vital service for that person. Sales can be noble profession.

In the Bible, Lydia was a sales rep. She sold purple goods, and selling purple was recognized and associated with royalty and nobility. Lydia was successful in her business, successful enough that she had a house large enough to hold her entire family. She would often invite guests to her home for dinner. Lydia was well respected in her circle of friends and with her family. We see in Acts 16 that when she opened her heart to the Lord, not only did she believe but her entire household also respected her and became believers. The Lord used a salesperson to bless Paul, Silas, and Timothy. The Lord blessed her, and she was able to bless Paul and others with generosity, generosity that was supplied by her job as a seller of fine purple dyes and linen. No matter what product or service you may be selling, when your approach is that of a true professional and understand that God may be using your service for "His" higher calling—sales is a noble profession.

How do you view your job in sales?

> Lord, thank You for providing for me through my sales efforts. Help me to be the best sales professional that I can be. Show me how You are using me and my sales for Your higher purpose. Thank You for providing for my sales today. Put people in my path that intend good and remove the people that mean harm. I'm depending on You to bring those prospective buyers. Thank You, Jesus.

ANXIOUS AND WORRIED

Rejoice in the Lord always; again I will say, rejoice. Let your reasonableness be known to everyone. The Lord is at hand; do not be anxious about anything, but in everything by prayer and supplication with thanksgiving let your requests be made known to God. And the peace of God, which surpasses all understanding, will guard your hearts and your minds in Christ Jesus.
—Philippians 4:4–7

Often in our sales role, we think that we are totally dependent upon ourselves for the outcome or results. We often ride the emotional sales rollercoaster, hanging our attitudes on each and every sale. Being anxious is often a signal that we are living in fear. Most salespeople are competitive by nature. They like to win and get extra satisfaction in closing a deal. When you're working with clients, when you have a sales quota and your performance or even your compensation is tied to closing a sale, there's naturally a certain amount of anxiousness that accompanies that. As a Christian, our value is not based upon each and every deal. Who we are in Christ is not a reflection of how much we are up or down in the quarter. Our value is based on the Lord and who we are in Christ. Being anxious and worrying can be a direct reflection of our trust in the Lord to provide.

Philippians tells us to not be anxious about anything and to bring everything to the Lord in prayer. The verse doesn't make the promise to help us close each and every deal, but it promises that we will have His peace, and He will guard our hearts and our minds *in* Christ Jesus. In Matthew 6:26, it says look at the birds in the air, they don't sow or reap, but the heavenly Father takes care of them, and you are much more valuable than the birds. Is it possible that your anxiety is directly related to your relationship with the Lord? Ask the

Lord to help show you the source of your worry and take that to Him in prayer.

Are you riding the emotional sales roller coaster? Do you need the peace that only God can offer?

> Lord, help me today to have the peace that only You can offer. Help me to not be anxious. Calm my heart today, Lord! Let me be grateful and thankful that You care about every aspect of my life! Thank You for caring about the smallest details in my life!

MAKE GOD A PART OF EVERYTHING WE DO

> In everything you do, put God first, and he will direct
> your path and crown your efforts with success.
> —Proverbs 3:6

I often hear individuals in the marketplace make statements like "I need to spend more time with God" or "I can't bring God into my business, or I might get fired." If Christ lives in us, we are already bringing God into the workplace. He is alive and resides in your heart already, so He goes with you everywhere you go. You also have the promised Holy Spirit that also goes with you everywhere you go. As a salesperson, we are constantly juggling schedules between demands with quotas, meeting customer deadlines, filling out reports, setting up appointments, driving, or flying to those appointments. This doesn't even include the time demands from family and kids activities or even sometime distractions from Church. The demands for our time can make us feel like we just don't have enough time to spend with the Lord.

The book of Proverbs says to put God first. If we feel like we can't spend more time with God, maybe we can strive to make God more of a part of everything we do? What are some ways we can make God a part of our everyday lives? Start out each and every day praying to be sensitive to who God puts in your path today. Spend time in the car in prayer; listen to Christian praise music between appointments. Perhaps listen to preaching podcasts or listening to the Word being read. Maybe it means just driving in silence to a meeting and listening to God. Pray for your customers in the parking lot before your meeting. Be sensitive to what your customers have going on in their personal lives. There may be opportunities to pray for something going on in their lives. I have a customer right now battling pancreatic cancer. As I write, I sent him a quick text to let him know that I am praying for him and had him on my mind. Ask God's blessings on your proposals, presentations, or meetings. Seek opportunities to pray for your coworkers and their families. Pray for your boss. Something way outside the normal way of thinking is praying for your competitors or the clients that you have conflict with. Pray for God to put people in your path that you can minister with. Always be quick to give God the praise for what he's doing in our lives. Acknowledge to God when a deal goes through. Thank God for the opportunities He is providing. We may not be able to carve out more time to spend with God, but if we make God a part of everything we do and acknowledge Him in every aspect of our lives, this puts God first and allows Him to direct our path.

Where are some areas that you can make God a part of your everyday life? How can you make God a part of your daily activities?

....

> God, thank You for the blessings of each and every day. Thank You for the way You provide even when I don't recognize it. I pray for my clients, my coworkers, my boss, and their families. Put people in my path that mean good and remove the people that intend harm. Help make me sensitive to Your Spirit in every aspect of my life! Thank You, Lord! Amen!

SHIPWRECKED

> Three times I was beaten with rods, one I was
> pelted with stones, three times I was shipwrecked,
> I spent a night and a day in the open sea.
> —2 Corinthians 11:25

Every sales representative will run into some rough "selling" seas at some point. You may even feel like you have been shipwrecked or pelted with stones a few times. Sales, at times, can be hard work. If you are a sales rep that works a territory by yourself, you can feel isolated and alone without any support. When you run into major resistance with an account, you start losing market share or even lose a major account, the feeling of being beaten and stoned can feel real. For anyone that has never experienced the pressure of meeting a sales quota or the company depending upon you for in-bound orders, the emotional feelings are real. There have been times in my sales life where I have lost a major account due to a change in the marketplace or variables that was out of my control. I can recall specific instances where a client replaced my company for little to no reason at all. The feeling of being shipwrecked was very real to me. The question that I must answer to God on a daily basis is, do I love Him, and do I trust Him? I do believe that God will protect me and has my best interest in mind?

In 2 Corinthians, Paul recounts the torture he's endured. Paul knew what it was like to be shipwrecked, beaten, stoned, constantly on the move, lived in danger, and gone without food and water. But Paul understood perseverance. He said in 2 Timothy 4:7, "I have fought the good fight, I have finished the race. I have kept the faith." Paul understood the depth of God's love for him, so in the midst of the storms, he stayed steadfast and strong. Paul goes on to say in 2 Corinthians 11:30, "If I must boast, I will boast of the things that show my weakness." It's in our weakness that God show's his faithfulness.

Has there been a time that you felt shipwrecked in the "selling" seas? Are you keeping the faith, fighting the good fight, and completing the race?

> Lord, thank You for helping me navigate through rough seas sometimes. Be with me today, bless my clients, bless my coworkers, and bless my competitors. Let me be quick to look for opportunities to be a faithful witness for You. Give me the endurance to complete the race and fight the good fight. Let any success or any failure I may have bring You glory and let me boast only in the Lord Jesus Christ. He shall be praised forever.

SMILE MORE

A cheerful look brings joy to the heart,
good news makes for good health.
—Proverbs 15:30

In the book *How to Make Friends and Influence People*, smiling is one of the key principles for impacting people. Happiness does not depend on our circumstances, but it is a reflection of our inward attitudes. Smiles are free to give and have an amazing ability to make others feel great as well. Smiling says "I am grateful for what God has done in my life." I have read studies that say 48 percent of being happy is in our DNA. It's how we are wired, but 52 percent of our happiness we can control. We control this by choosing to be optimistic, upbeat, positive, and happy. When we smile, we send a signal to our brain that says "If I'm smiling, something good must be happening," and it releases endorphins in our brain. Often our outlook becomes one of ungratefulness. In the world of sales, there are often times the pressure is real, the disappointment of losing a sale hurts, the internal conflict between operations and sales exists, but we should not let these situations or circumstances bring us spiraling down. Happy is contagious, just as a dejected person can bring someone else down. Customers like to buy from people that are positive, upbeat, and happy.

Solomon, in the book of Ecclesiastes, tells us there is a time to weep; but he also says there is a time to laugh and a time to dance. In the book of Proverbs, it says a cheerful look brings joy to the heart. Not only does smiling bring health benefits such as lower blood pressure, relieve stress, put you in a better mood; it also sends a signal to your brain that something good is happening. Constantly responding with a negative attitude is often a reflection of losing sight of God's goodness and what he's done for us. In the morning before you get out of bed, say a prayer of thankfulness to God and practice smiling. It will start your day off by telling your brain that you have something to smile about. So the next time that negative email comes in, the exhaustive conference call happens, production has lead time issues, you can't meet the required price, you have a bad performance review, you have an upset customer, or that driver cuts you off heading to your next appointment; choose happy and smile! It's contagious!

Have you allowed your circumstances to determine your happiness?

> Lord, thank You for the blessings You provide to me every day. Thank You for the way You provide that I take for granted. Help me to smile more today. You give me reasons to smile every day. Forgive me for taking those things for granted. Let me be a light to others around me. Let me choose happy today! Thank You, Lord! Amen!

BE DIVERSE

Invest in seven ventures, yes, in eight; you do not know what disaster may come upon the land.
—Ecclesiastes 11:2

I once worked for a company that 95 percent of its total revenue came from one customer. This was a very dangerous position to be in. When I was hired, I was given the task to diversify our revenue and create greater balance in our income stream. This decision became timely as, ultimately, the customer shifted a majority of their work to another vendor. Had we have not been proactive, we would have been left in an extremely vulnerable position that would have more than likely led to closing the business. We all know of companies that once upon a time had dominant names in their particular industries only to have the market shift, leaving them in a helpless state and ultimately bankrupt.

Ecclesiastes tells us to invest in multiple ventures because we do not know what disaster may come. Some would say having a backup plan is not trusting in the Lord, but Ecclesiastes is not saying to live in fear but rather diversify. God has wired you with knowledge, and the Bible is providing guidance to have balance to not put all your eggs in one basket. In the world of sales, how can we be more diverse? This may mean having balance in our business plans. Have revenue that comes from multiple products or cuts across various vertical markets or business units. Within a customer, we should have relationships that are three-by-three—that is, three wide and three deep. Get to know their organizational chart and form those relationships. The above verse is really talking about having balance in our lives, with our work, with our family, with our Church, and with our customers; but within our sales role, we need to be diverse and have a balanced strategy.

Are you balanced in your life? What steps do you need to take to create diversity in your work and with your family?

....

> Lord, help me today to build deeper and more meaningful relationships. In areas where I am vulnerable, help introduce new contacts. Help me to see where I need to be more diverse and create balance. Thank You for showing me this simple truth! Amen!

HARD WORK

All hard work brings a profit, but mere
talk leads only to poverty.
—Proverbs 14:23

As a sales rep, having a good work ethic is vital. You may often be working alone, from a home office, or covering a large territory with little daily oversight. In order to have success, it becomes imperative to be self-motivated and have a good work routine. The Bible says in 2 Thessalonians 3:10 that if you're not willing to work, then you shouldn't eat. This may not be a popular theme today, but you may have to be honest with yourself and say, "If I'm not working hard, should I feel entitled to the nicer things?" This message was probably not a popular message even in the days when Paul traveled with Silas and Timothy to minister in Thessalonica. Proverbs tells us that all hard work brings a profit. So ask yourself, "Am I putting forth the effort that is required to reach the results that I desire?" Colossians 3:23 says, "Whatever you do, work at it with all your heart, as working for the Lord, not for human masters."

Purchase orders and sales are a by-product of hard work. We are often judged according to the revenue we bring into a company, but sales are simply an indicator of the activities you've been putting forth. So if sales are simply a result of our efforts, then how should we measure a productive day? I call it the Work Watchers program. Each day, you should achieve a specific point total. Points are allocated for setting an appointment, attending an appointment, working with a complimentary partner, making a cold call, etc. Activities equal results. In the end, the results are up to the Lord. John Adams spent twenty-eight years working and consistently fighting for the emancipation of slaves. A reporter once asked Adams why he kept pushing for emancipation when it seemed hopeless. Adams looked at the reporter and said simply, "Duty is ours, results are God's" and then walked away. It just so happens that Adams mentored a young legislator that eventually had a big impact on the emancipation of slaves. Adams ended up passing away after twenty-eight years of serving, but that young man's name that Adams mentored was Abraham Lincoln. Results are up to God. Proverbs 16:33 says, "The lot is cast into the lap, but its every decision is from the Lord."

Do your current efforts equal your desired results? If not, what changes can you make today to help increase your productivity?

....

> Thank You, Lord, for constantly providing for me. You supply all my needs. Lord, You understand my sales quotas, goals, and expectations that are set before me. Thank You for reminding me that my work is for You, and the results are up to You. Put the right prospects in my path. Thank You that You are faithful, and I can depend on You to help me today! Amen!

THIS I KNOW

> So for the second time they called the man who had been blind and said to him, "Give glory to God. We know that this man is a sinner." He answered, "Whether he is a sinner I do not know. One thing I do know, that though I was blind, now I see."
>
> —John 9:24–25

The best endorsement you can have is that of a happy and satisfied customer. You can spend enormous amounts of money on magnificent marketing campaigns only to have someone try a product, and the hype doesn't live up to the actual product. Nothing beats an authentic satisfied-customer testimony. One of the best projects that I ever sold came from a positive endorsement from a similar customer. In this particular case, one of my prospective customers was looking to install our highest-priced and highest-performing products. We went through the typical sales cycle of demonstrating the product, providing technical support, discussing the various value propositions and eventually working through budget discussions. The customer was still undecided due to the fact the product they were considering was beyond what they had budgeted and had prepared for. What ended up closing the deal for us was when she reached out to a similar customer that had already installed these products. The customer gave us a glowing review. Nothing we could have said would have convinced them the same as a customer that was very pleased with their decision.

In John 9, Jesus heals a man that had been blind since birth. Jesus performed this miracle on the Sabbath day, which angered some of the religious elites. Later, the Pharisees brought the man that had been blind before them to question him. They pressed him for an answer: "How did Jesus do this?" They even questioned his parents, and they quickly responded, "He is old enough, ask him yourself." So they questioned him again and this is when he gave a raving testimony. "One thing I know, I was blind and now I see," he said. How can they argue with that? The blind man was so pleased with the miracle that Jesus had performed, he would risk being persecuted to provide a testimony of the amazing work. When you have a customer that is so pleased with you, your product, your performance, your company, their testimony will mean more than any words you can say. How many times for yourself when maybe you've been completely satisfied or even impressed with a service, price, product, or solution that you've told all your friends, family, and anyone that will listen how great it was?

Who are some of your best customers that would provide a tremendous case study? If you know you are underperforming or overstating and underdelivering, how can you make the necessary changes?

....

> Dear heavenly Father, thank You once again for showing me areas that I need to improve. Help me to be transparent, humble, and sincere in providing solutions for my customers. Direct me to the customers that are completely satisfied with our service and my abilities and would sincerely provide a positive referral. Thank You for caring about the smallest details of my life, including my ability to provide through my job in sales.

DON'T CUT CORNERS

When the master of the feast tasted the water now become wine, and did not know where it came from (though the servants who had drawn the water knew), the master of the feast called the bridegroom and said to him, "Everyone serves the good wine first, and when people have drunk freely, then the poor wine. But you have kept the good wine until now."
—John 2:9–10

Put forth your very best effort every time. The story of Jesus turning water into wine is the very first recorded miracle in the Bible. Jesus was attending a wedding with his friends and family. At the request of his mother Mary, Jesus instructs the servants to take the jugs and fill them with water. He could have stopped there and say, "Hey, sorry, it's not my job." He could have easily made some poor-tasting wine as it sounds like everyone was accustomed to doing at a wedding. Jesus didn't cut corners. He not only made wine so the bridegroom would not be embarrassed; he made the very best wine. What's fascinating, ask any wine maker and the very best wine is aged. Jesus cut right through the aging process and made the finest tasting wine. He provided a product that was better than the master of the feast had originally provided.

In the course of sales, we can often decide to cut corners. When a customer asks for extreme discounts, we can attempt to match the price by cutting corners, completing a poor installation, eliminating some process that decreases the quality. Jesus provided an example of not cutting corners. Provide the best service, best quality, best product, best installation, best performance, and provide excellent value to the customer. You may say, "Our customer will not pay for quality. They view our product or service as a commodity." That may be true but you as a sales professional can still provide the best representation possible. Treat your customers no matter how much they buy or how little they buy with the best service possible. I often say, if a customer has a choice and they are buying my product and it's 100 percent up to them, I don't care if the widget is the least valued product in our catalogue, I'm going to make sure they know that I appreciate it!

Are you cutting corners anywhere with your product or service? Are you letting your customers know how much you appreciate and value their business?

....

> My Lord and Savior Jesus Christ, thank You for your grace and mercy. Speak to me in a clear, audible voice. Illuminate in my heart areas that I need to be sensitive to. Help me to put forth my very best effort. Remind me to be thankful for my customers. Provide for my customers and bless their business and their lives.

EXCEED YOUR CUSTOMERS EXPECTATIONS

> And they all ate and were satisfied. And they took up the twelve baskets full of the broken pieces left over. And those who ate were about five thousand men, besides women and children.
> —Matthew 14:20–21

"Underpromise and overdeliver" is a statement that is often overly used in the sales world, but it remains more valid in today's business climate than ever before. In a world where there's more competition than ever, exceeding customer expectations is a must. Going above and beyond your customers' expectations is one of the easiest ways to retain and radiate a customer. Most sales experts will say it's much easier to provide additional services or products to an existing customer than trying to go out and land a brand-new client. It cost five times as much to attract a new customer than to keep an existing one. Fifty percent of existing satisfied customers are willing to try a new product, and they are willing to spend 31 percent more. One customer experience agency found loyal customers are five times as likely to forgive, five times as likely to repurchase, four times as likely to refer, and seven times as likely to try a new offering. Would you agree? So if retaining an existing customer is important, how do we do that? We have to exceed our customers' expectations.

In Matthew chapter 14, the Bible records a story of Jesus feeding five thousand people. Jesus had gone to a remote area, and because of his preaching, He had huge crowds that were following, listening, and learning from him. Matthew says He showed them compassion and was healing the sick. Granted, these are not Jesus's customers, but they were followers of his teachings. The Bible says it became evening, and the crowds had no place to go or anything to eat. That's when Jesus said to his disciples, "We need to feed them."

The recorded miracle says the disciples brought five loaves and two fish to Jesus. Jesus took the loaves and bread, blessed it, and it multiplied. Not only did he feed the five thousand–plus, but he also had twelve baskets of excess. Jesus exceeded any expectations that day. Jesus didn't just feed them and meet their physical need; He exceeded their expectations by feeding them more than they could even eat. He also fed them the "living" Word. Their lives were changed forever! The crowd was physically fed and spiritually fed. Now that's exceeding the customer's expectations!

So what are some practical ways we can exceed a customer's expectations? Start off by doing what we say we are going to do! Not only should delivering a quality product be a given today, but also making sure the product is exactly what the customer ordered. Matthew 5:37 says, "Let what you say be simply 'Yes' or 'No'"; anything more than this comes from evil." Simply put, be honest! When you make a commitment, keep it. Do everything within your power to meet any delivery deadlines. Show additional value beyond what the customer expected and beyond price.

What are some unexpected things that you could do for your customers?

....

> Jesus, thank You for giving us examples of how you exceeded expectations. Thank You for providing for our needs, and thank You for providing for our salvation through the cross. We give you praise for all of our blessings. We give You praise for providing for our daily lives. Thank You, Jesus!

FOUR ANCHORS OF SALES: PERSISTENCE (STEADFASTNESS), PATIENCE, INTEGRITY, AND ATTITUDE

> Fearing that we would be dashed against
> the rocks, they dropped four anchors from
> the stern and prayed for daylight.
> —Acts 27:29

The book of Acts tells a story of Paul drifting in the Adriatic Sea in the middle of a storm when the ship he was aboard was about to crash into land. Acts 27:29 says that they determined how deep the water was and they dropped four anchors and then prayed for daylight. The sales storms are going to happen. When they do, what is your course of action? Sometimes when you find yourself in the midst of a "sales storm," praying for daylight may appear to be the only solution. Prayer is always our best course of action.

What is interesting is despite being in the middle of a life-threatening storm, Paul remained confident. Where did this confidence come from? His confidence came from the Lord. In verses 23–25, Acts says an angel of the Lord had appeared to Paul and told him, "Don't be afraid, Paul. You must stand before Caesar. Therefore, take courage!" His confidence came from his dependence upon the Lord!

What are the four anchors for a good sales rep? The four anchors for any successful sales rep must be remaining persistent, being patient, always operating with integrity, and maintaining a good attitude.

So when you find yourself in that sales storm, have confidence in the Lord. Continue to pray for daylight and drop your four anchors: Be persistent, be patient, continue to operate with integrity, and maintain a good attitude!

....

> Father, thank You that in the middle of any storm in life, I can depend on You. You are my ultimate anchor, and in You I put my trust. Help me to maintain a good attitude and strengthen me as I remain patient, persistent, and help me to make the right choices with integrity! Thank You that I can come to You in prayer, and I can trust You to protect me from any of life's storms!

PERSISTENCE

And he told them a parable to the effect that they ought always to pray and not lose heart. He said, "In a certain city there was a judge who neither feared God nor respected man. And there was a widow in that city who kept coming to him and saying, 'Give me justice against my adversary.' For a while he refused, but afterward he said to himself, 'Though I neither fear God nor respect man, yet because this widow keeps bothering me, I will give her justice, so that she will not beat me down by her continual coming."
—Luke 18:1–8

Benjamin Franklin once said, "Energy and persistence conquers all things." Every sales rep must possess knowledge, but I would dare say knowledge without persistence will leave you empty-handed. Persistence is the continuance in a course of action in spite of difficulty or opposition. We have all had those meetings that when you leave, you're handing out high fives because you had all the buy signals, only to have the deal fall apart before a purchase order was signed. I would love to have a signed purchase order after every meeting. That's just not reality. In order to be a successful sales rep, you must possess the ability to be persistent.

I have a large financial institution as a recent, new customer. Over the years, I have responded to several requests for pricing, conducted numerous presentations, sampled products, entertained them, and struck out every time. Only after years of striking out did I finally find an open door. The opportunity actually came after having a conversation with the customer where I recapped all the bid opportunities on numerous products that we had lost over the years and finally said, "What can we talk about?" That is when he told me where he had an interest. With that simple question, he helped guide me to a path of being able to do business with his company. Persistence is what opened the opportunity.

Luke 18 tells a story of the persistent widow. In her case, she was seeking justice against her adversary. The story says the judge eventually granted her justice due to her persistence. The story says the judge granted her justice so she would quit bothering him. Now, I don't recommend "bothering" a client to the point they get a restraining order against you and ban you from their office, but the lesson of persistence with consistent, actionable follow-up is vital.

Are there any prospective clients that you have perhaps given up on? Do you need to make a list of those target accounts and renew your purpose in calling on them?

> Lord, thank You for being a God that cares about the smallest details of my life. I acknowledge that every good and perfect gift is from You. Bring to my mind the clients that I need to call on. Put people in my path that intend good for me and remove the people that intend harm. I praise You for the blessings You have given me, and I thank You for the way You will provide. You are Jehovah Jireh—the great provider! Thank You for Your provisions! In Jesus's name I pray. Amen!

PATIENCE

*And let us not grow weary of doing good, for in
due season we will reap, if we do not give up.*
—Galatians 6:9

I have heard it says that God answers every prayer—either yes, no, or whoa! Quite often in sales, regardless of how much we push the answer is not yet. So what is the difference between persistence and patience? If persistence is the ability to push and keep pushing through until you see a result, then patience is having the capacity to accept or tolerate a delay without getting angry or upset. Sometimes no matter how hard or how much we push, the answer is wait. I like the word *fortitude*. We must exercise fortitude. What is fortitude? *Fortitude* is defined as courage in pain or adversity. We must wait patiently and let God work out the details.

Often in the times of waiting, that's when we feel God is being silent. It becomes more imperative than ever to claim to God's word for truth. We must remember that in God's word, it says that love is patient in 1 Corinthians 13. We must cling to the promise that if we wait patiently, God will renew our strength if we wait on the Lord in Isaiah 40 and in Psalm 37, to be still before the Lord and wait patiently for him. This is hard to do. As a sales rep, we like to see progress; we like to get results and the companies that we work for demand results. After all, if you are in sales, you are measured on the results of purchase orders and sales. If in your mind you have done everything you can possibly do, then the situation requires you to exercise fortitude and have the courage to wait. Often, we are quick to immediately lower our price or offer a deeper discount thinking this will bring an immediate result. That may be the appropriate strategy, but often, it can backfire and create more doubt in the customers' eye. They may think, "Why didn't you offer that price to begin with?" More often, we must remain calm, exercise patience, and let God do the work. One thing to keep in mind, when you exercise patience and you see God's faithfulness, make a mental marker and remember this in the future.

Can you recall times when you exercised patience and saw God's faithfulness? Are there some customers that come to your mind and the best course of action is to wait?

> God, thank You for Your faithfulness. Thank You for fighting my battles. You are my shield, my fortress, and my King. Help me to remain patient and fight the temptation to take matters into my own hand. Thank You for providing. Bring to my mind the times in the past that You helped me and let me never forget. Thank You for loving me! In Jesus's name I pray! Amen!

INTEGRITY

> For we aim at what is honorable not only in the
> Lord's sight but also in the sight of man.
> —2 Corinthians 8:21

If everyone lived by the golden rule of "do unto others as you would have done to you," then integrity would be an easy choice. The problem is we often live with a motto that's more like "do unto others as they have done to you." Integrity is the reflection of our character. The true test of our character is what we choose to do when no one is watching. We often justify our actions by making statements like "That's just the culture of my industry" or "I'm not lying. I'm just stretching the truth a little bit," or maybe "That's what my competitors do. If it's okay for them, then it's okay for me."

Matthew 5:37 says, "Let your yes be yes and your no be no for whatever is more than these is from the evil one." Integrity is having the courage to take a stand no matter the consequences. In our sales role, the dreaded quota always seems to be peeking out from behind the door. Often in the pressure of trying to "make the sale," we feel compelled to compromise our integrity, make the moral poor choice, or choose to remain silent. Proverbs 14:12 says, "There is a way that seem right to man but in the end leads to death." As a follower of Christ, we are and should be called to a higher standard. When we compromise our integrity, we are in essence saying, "Lord, I trust my ways more than I trust you. I don't trust you to take care of me." Today, choose the better way. Choose integrity! Identify areas where you have compromised your integrity and make a dedicated choice now to stop and change!

Are there areas in your life that you are compromising your integrity? Can you identify those areas where you know you have lowered your moral standard? Ask God to forgive you?

....

> Dear heavenly Father, today I choose integrity. I place my whole trust in You to provide. In You alone will I look for my provisions. Illuminate the areas of my life where I have compromised my integrity. Forgive me, Lord! Amen!

ATTITUDE

> In the same way, let your light shine before others,
> so that they may see your good works and give
> glory to your Father who is in heaven.
> —Matthew 5:16

Keeping a good attitude at work can be extremely difficult. Most sales jobs are dealing with rejection the majority of the time. Even the best sales rep never closes 100 percent of every opportunity. Negativity is part of the job. Sometimes, we may see the lack of leadership coming from our managers; we may see where our companies could make simple improvements to help us close more deals or lack confidence in leadership to make the right choices. Other times, perhaps we've done everything right and operations can't deliver. Most organizations are not sales-driven but operations-driven. They look at things a completely different way than a sales rep would. This creates the constant friction and conflict between sales and ops. It can be hard to maintain motivation and keep a positive attitude in this kind of environment, not to mention we have a quota to hit. If you're like me and your love language is words of affirmation, you may feel like your company doesn't even speak that language. Maintaining a good attitude can be a real challenge, and it requires tons of effort.

So how do we keep a good attitude even in the midst of these challenges? It begins with having a higher purpose than simply closing a deal. We must view our sales jobs as a mission field. We may be the only person a customer or coworker sees that serves as a reflection of Christ in their lives. Matthew 5:16 says our light should shine before others so they may see Christ in you and give glory to the heavenly Father. When we start thinking each day about who God may put in our life, it can help start the day with a different attitude. Second, we must choose to put on a good attitude. Daniel 1:8 says that Daniel purposed in his heart to not defile himself. Daniel made a choice. We must strive to "purpose" in our hearts to have a good attitude.

What are some areas where you have a bad attitude? Think about this list and purpose in your heart today to make changes. Ask God to help refresh your attitude today.

> Father of heaven, today let me choose a good attitude. Let me be a reflection of Your goodness and kindness. Show me areas where I need to improve my attitude. Let me view my job as my mission field. Put people in my path today that will offer affirmation. Thank You for loving me in spite of my bad attitude. In Jesus's name I pray. Amen.

WALK IN INTEGRITY

Whoever walks in integrity walks securely, but he who makes his ways crooked will be found out.
—Proverbs 10:9

I work in an industry that tests your integrity daily by the sheer nature of the way our industry is structured. At any moment, I may be providing pricing on a bid with multiple contractors, and they are working with multiple distributors while my main competitors are working with the same people. Often, they will position one against the other in order to drive the price lower and turn it into a bidding war with the lowest price winning. There is often an overwhelming sensation or temptation to lie or deceive in order to secure the business. It forces you to make a choice to operate with integrity each day. The very nature of our business can challenge your moral choices. Perhaps you have the same challenges in your sales role? Maybe you feel the internal pressure to succeed or to win, and you may be telling yourself it's okay to compromise your integrity on this one deal.

The Bible tells us Solomon was a king with amazing wealth. He prayed for wisdom in 1 Kings, and God granted that prayer. Solomon known as a king who had tremendous wisdom. Solomon wrote in Proverbs 10:9 that whoever walks in integrity walks securely, but he also says if your ways are crooked, you will be found out. He says in the next verse that a babbling fool will come to ruin.

You may be tempted to compromise your integrity. Is it worth it? You may close that one deal, but will you do any additional business with that customer when they find out? Probably not. Proverbs 10:18 says the wages of the righteous leads to life!

Dear heavenly Father, You are the great provider and source of wisdom. Help me today to choose integrity. Let me walk in Your faithfulness and lead me to the path of righteousness. I confess that sometimes I feel the temptation to take matters into my own hands and make unwise decisions. Help me to trust You for all my decisions. I acknowledge that You are in control. Thank You, Father and my Lord!

GAIN THE WHOLE WORLD!

> For what shall it profit a man, if he shall gain
> the whole world, and lose his own soul?
> —Mark 8:36

What does Whitney Houston, Michael Jackson, Robin Williams, and Ernest Hemingway all have in common? They all had success but tragically passed away. It is commonly known that all battled from depression even though they were amazingly successful, wealthy, and famous. In your sales role, you may be the top performer every year but still be unsatisfied and unfulfilled. I have a friend who received the global sales award for a major communications provider. He was number 1 in the world for this company, but when he got there, he realized the sacrifices he had made did not equal the pleasure or fulfillment that he hoped for by attaining this goal.

The book of Mark says what does it profit a man to gain the whole world but lose his own soul? Proverbs 14:23 says that all hard work brings a profit, and 2 Thessalonians says if a person does not work, they shall not eat. So the Bible is clear that we should work hard. There is nothing wrong with setting goals and praying for God's guidance in achieving those goals. But if your drive for achievement rules over all other aspects of your life, then you may end up with the feeling of loneliness and emptiness once you get there.

So how do you lose your soul? Salvation comes through Jesus Christ alone! First Corinthians 15:3–4 says that Christ died for our sins, and He was buried and rose again on the third day. If you confess your sins to God and put your trust in Jesus Christ, God will forgive you and you will be saved!

Work hard. Yes, set goals. Yes, achieve success. Yes…but do not lose your soul!

Do you have the proper perspective of success in your life? Take a minute and really ask if you are placing your trust in Christ?

....

> Jesus, I come to You today. I confess that I have failed You and have sinned against You. I ask You for forgiveness. Thank You for paying my penalty on the cross, and thank You that your life promises me eternal life! Be with me today. Let me live my life for You. Any success that I have, let me give You the glory! In the name of the Father, Jesus Christ, and the Holy Ghost, amen!

LET YOUR YES BE YES

All you need to say is simply "Yes" or "No";
anything beyond this comes from the evil one.
—Matthew 5:37

We live in a time that many people have a mindset that if something can't be proven in a court of law beyond a shadow of doubt, then it must not have happened. We justify our actions by saying it depends on what the definition or the application of a word means at the time to determine if I'm guilty or not.

My dad used to tell me that as long as you tell him the truth, he would defend me till the end. That was a comforting statement and one that I tell my boys often as well, but if I'm being honest, then I should tell the truth to everyone, not just my dad when I'm in trouble. Matthew tells us that our yes should be yes, and our no should be no. Our answer should not be determined by the situation. We should always lead with truth.

I know of companies whose part of their strategy is to enter into a contract knowing there was mistakes in the original submittal then bill the customer for change orders and then potentially fight the dispute out in a court. As little kids, we are taught the phrase by Sir Walter Scott: "Oh, what a tangled web we weave when first we practice to deceive!" As a sales professional, we should strive to always tell the truth. Lead with integrity and let our yes be yes and no be no!

Are there areas in your business or personal life that you are willing to compromise the truth?

Lord, thank You for this day You have given me. Sometimes I take it for granted the very air that I breath. Help guide me and lead me today.

Show me areas where I may be compromising the truth. Always let my word be my bond. Help me to walk in integrity and be the light that points people to You. Thank You for blessing me! Amen!

GRUMBLING

> Do all things without grumbling or questioning, that you may be blameless and innocent, children of God without blemish in the midst of a crooked and twisted generation, among whom you shine as lights of the world.
> —Philippians 2:14–15

I am the king of moaning and groaning. Just ask my wife. As sales reps, we are constantly grumbling, complaining, or questioning things. Sales initiatives, quota', pricing, lead times, the direction of the company, operational support, lack of stock, product gaps, implementation, lack of leadership, lazy coworkers, product defects, conference calls, slow-paying customers, competitor tactics, our territory, our compensation plan, and the list goes on and on. Most sales reps that I have met can make a sport out of complaining. In some cases, our observations may be true and have merit. Often, our complaining is a true reflection of our own internal attitudes. You may be facing real job burnout. Stay in a job long enough, and everyone will go through waves or periods of peaks and valleys. The real question is what is the real source of our groaning? Is it pride, self, or a lack of thankfulness? Philippians 2 says, "Do all things without grumbling," and why? So we may be blameless and innocent, children of God.

If you are facing true job burnout, call a timeout, take some time away, and really reflect and get alone with the Lord. I have found in those "burnout" times; if I recognize that it's coming on and take some time off, get away and perhaps can spend some time alone in prayer and reflecting with the Lord, I come back more motivated. Be able to recognize true burnout. If, however, your complaining is coming from a place of self-centered thoughts, be aware and own this. Confess before the Lord your true feelings and ask him to show you areas that need worked on. We need to own the grumbling and complaining and call it what it is. Perhaps we need to make a list of everything that we are thankful for and reflect on this list. Call it your praise list. Go on the blessing walk and give God the glory for all the good things he has done. I think if you will do this, you will quickly find yourself nipping the negative thoughts in the bud and shining as lights unto the world. Second Corinthians 2:15 says we are a sweet aroma or fragrance to God. Let our words be a sweet aroma to God and to others.

Are there areas in your life and job that you are constantly complaining? Has grumbling and questioning become a sport for you? Make a list today of the areas where you are complaining and ask God to help you in those areas.

> Sweet heavenly Father, let me words be a pleasing aroma to You. Show me where the areas of my life that I am complaining, groaning, and questioning others. I ask You to give me a heart of thankfulness. Let my attitudes reflect Your glory and be a light to others! Thank You, Jesus! Amen!

HARSH WORDS

> A gentle answer turns away wrath, but
> a harsh word stirs up anger.
> —Proverbs 15:1

No doubt if you stay in sales long enough, you will have numerous hard conversations. Although conflict may not be completely unavoidable, we should strive to avoid words that create anger. Proverbs 15:1 says, "A harsh word stirs up anger but a gentle answer turns away wrath."

I recently sat down and tried to recall everyone that I have had harsh words with throughout my sales career. On this list were coworkers, former customers, and other vendor partners. Unfortunately, that list was much longer than I wished it was. In some cases, I was able to go back to that person and restore the relationship. In some situations, restoration was not possible, but I still needed to confess my actions before the Lord and ask God for forgiveness. In my case and in some situations, I had allowed bitterness and resentment to build up in me as a result of the previous conflict. Ephesians 4 says to get rid of all bitterness and anger, and we are to be kind and compassionate to one another. We need to strive to replace harsh words that leads to anger and bitterness with compassion. Hebrews 12 says to make every effort to live in peace and make sure no bitter root grows up inside you.

Are there relationships that need to be restored? Have you allowed a root of bitterness to grow up inside you? Perhaps you may need to make that list and work on restoration where possible?

Lord, I confess to You that I don't always lead with compassion. I have allowed harsh words to create conflict with coworkers, clients, friends, family, and others. I ask for Your forgiveness where I have bitterness and resentment. I ask for You to restore relationships where possible. I ask for You to create a renewed spirit inside me. Thank You for being a loving, kind Father. Now, help me to go out today and be a light for You. Help me to show love and kindness and to conduct my business in a way that would glorify Your name. In the precious name of Jesus I pray! Amen!

PRAISE

Through him then let us continually offer up a sacrifice of praise to God, that is, the fruit of lips that acknowledge his name.
—Hebrews 13:15

Do you offer up praise to God every time you get a sale, purchase order, signed contract, or close a deal? I get a visual image that when we offer up a praise to God, a bell goes off in heaven. Now keep in mind, God doesn't need our praise like it's a tip jar bell going off, but we should be acknowledging His name for every good deed that occurs in our life. This includes when we make a sale. This is an easy way to include God in everything we do and truly acknowledge who's in control. James 1:7 says that every good and perfect gift is from above, coming down from the Father of heavenly lights. Our praise is a direct reflection of our beliefs in God being in control. Do we think it's our actions and we are self-sufficient, or do we believe that God is in control of our lives?

Next time you close a deal, offer up to the Lord a praise and acknowledgment for his provisions. Hebrews 13 says our praise is fruit of the lips. Nothing is better than perfectly ripened fresh fruit. That's what our praise is to God.

Start acknowledging God for every sale you make!

> Gracious Lord, thank You for being a God that is in control of every aspect of my life. I have not always acknowledged You in my sales life. Thank You for providing. Thank You for the sales that You have given to me. I ask for Your continued help and want my praise to be a sweet sacrifice to You. I love You, Lord. In Jesus's sweet name I pray! Amen!

GIVE ME THAT MOUNTAIN

> I am still as strong today as I was the day Moses sent me out. My strength for battle and for daily tasks is now as it was then. Now give me this hill country the Lord has promised me on that day, because you heard then that the Anakim are there, as well as large fortified cities. Perhaps the Lord will be with me and I will drive them out as the Lord promised.
> —Joshua 14:11–12

The Bible mentions a person named Caleb that was an absolute warrior. At eighty-five years old, he showed no fear when he approached Joshua and reminded him of the Lord's promise that he was to inherit the land of Hebron. Joshua records the land of Hebron had Anakim. The Anakim that is mentioned in the Bible were considered to be giants. Hebron also had large, fortified, and well-protected cities not to mention the fact that Caleb was a senior citizen when he approached Joshua. The King James translation also says Hebron was a mountain. So at eighty-five years old, Caleb is ready to face giants, large, fortified cities, and conquer a mountain to gain the land he had been promised. Now that's a warrior mentality!

So, the question becomes, what are the "giants" you are facing? What appears to be a "fortified city" that is standing in your way? What are the "mountains" you have to conquer? You may be at a point in your sales career that you think there's just no hope or no potential. It may appear that some accounts are so well protected there's no way you'll ever be able to penetrate them. Maybe you think you're getting too old, you're underqualified or the task at hand is just way too big. Caleb serves as a reminder that as long as the Lord is on our side, we are never too old, accounts are never too big, or territories are never too protected to conquer. Joshua 14:14 says, "Hebron became the inheritance of Caleb to this day." Hebron belongs to

Caleb because he wholly followed the Lord! Victory belonged to Caleb, and victory can belong to you!

What are the mountains you are facing? What are the Giants standing in your way? What are the obstacles and challenges that you face today? Bring that list before the Lord in prayer and ask God to stand with you.

....

> Lord, thank You for helping me in battle. Thank You for being a God that never grows tired. You are a good, good Father! I humbly come before You and ask that You help me face what appears to be giants in my life. I praise You for helping me conquer protected territories. I pray for strength, guidance, and direction. Make my paths straight! Help me have a warrior mentality. You are my protector! In Jesus's precious name I pray. Amen!

DUST OFF YOUR FEET

> And if anyone will not receive you or listen to
> your words, shake off the dust from your feet
> when you leave that house or town.
> —Matthew 10:14

When Jesus sent the twelve disciples out, He told them to go into the town and to proclaim the kingdom of heaven is at hand. He told them to heal the sick, raise the dead, cleanse lepers, and cast out demons. Interesting enough, He also said if they entered a house, and they received resistance or wasn't welcome to simply shake the dust off their feet and to move on. Jesus is discussing intentional evangelism with His disciples here, but there's also real sales principle that applies.

There may be those occasions when we need to pass on an opportunity, move on from continuing pursuing a prospect, or "fire" the customer. There's an opportunity cost that is associated with every minute you spend with a customer that down deep you know is never going to buy anything from you. In certain situations, when you've done all you can possible do or you have a client that you need to "let go," sometimes it may require that as a sales rep, you shake the dust off our feet, and we move on. As a professional sales rep, we never like to give up or accept the thought that we lost a deal. We are programmed to win and to keep fighting till the bitter end. But continuing to pursue a client when it's a dead end is not only wasting your time but potentially limiting your time to pursue a prospective client that is open and receptive to what you have to say. In some of these cases, it may make better sense to withdraw, regroup, wait for a change in their organization or some new message from your own company, and then reengage. The longer you keep pursuing, the further away you get from making the sale. You get frustrated, the customer is agitated, and no progress is being made. In those cases, shake the dust off your feet, stay focused, and move on.

Are there some customers that you need to move on from?

....

> Lord, You are a God of perfect timing. You know my every step. Thank You for putting on my heart when I should move on or when I should stay engaged. You make the plans for me. It's in You that I trust! Show me, tell me, and teach me when to stay focused on a customer and when to move on. Thank You, Jesus! Amen!

ABIDE IN ME

> Abide in me, and I in you. As the branch cannot bear fruit by itself, unless it abides in the vine, neither can you, unless you abide in me. I am the vine; you are the branches. Whoever abides in me and I in him, he it is that bears much fruit, for apart from me you can do nothing.
> —John 15:4–5

I have a tree in my backyard. It was struck by lightning several years ago, and it's slowly dying from the inside out. For now, every year, the leaves continue to blossom, even though the inside is decaying. Why is this? Well, the root system is still intact and the top of the tree is still attached to the roots. As long as the branches remain attached to the root system, and it continues to get water, it will continue to blossom. In John 15, Jesus speaks to his disciples and uses an example of a vine and branch. He tells his disciples that a tree will continue to bear fruit as long as it stays connected to the vine. Jesus is the vine, and we are the branches. Jesus is saying to remain in Him, abide in Him, trust in Him, depend on Him. Stay attached, and we will bear fruit; try to do it on our own, and we will wither and die.

Too often in sales, we want to think we are in this by ourselves. We want to go it alone. When we have success, we did it. When we have failures, someone else did it. What Jesus is saying to his disciples applies to us in our sales profession as well. Abide in him. He's saying, "Trust Me with this." Sales are going well. "Abide in Me." Sales are down. "Abide in Me." Should I change jobs? "Abide in Me." Should I take a promotion? "Abide in Me." I'm having a challenge with a customer. "Abide in Me." I'm having conflict with a coworker. "Abide in Me." Should I retire? "Abide in Me." What Jesus is saying is to "abide in Me for every aspect of our lives," and this includes our sales profession. And what does he say in verse 5 if we abide in Him? We will bear much fruit! So I encourage you today. Abide in Him!

What area of your life are you trying to do on your own? Confess to Jesus now that where you have tried to separate from the true vine and ask Him to forgive you.

....

> Jesus, thank You for being the true vine. Thank You for being my Savior. Thank You for caring about every aspect of my life. I ask You to be with me in every detail of my job, my family, and my life. Holy Spirit, help me to remain in Him! Thank You for promising to provide! In the name of Jesus I pray. Amen!

SING PRAISE

Let the word of Christ dwell in you richly,
teaching and admonishing one another in wisdom,
singing psalms and hymns and spiritual songs,
with thankfulness in your hearts to God.
—Colossians 3:16

It has been said, the easiest time to close a sale is right after you have sold something. Why is this? We are so filled with excitement from the sale, we can use this energy and transfer the enthusiasm into the next sales call. With the success of a new sale, it is a good reminder to take that overwhelming excitement we are experiencing and offer up a praise immediately. By immediately offering up praise, we acknowledge where the true source of the sale is coming from—God. Our praise removes our "self or I did it" focus and instead gives us a heart of thankfulness. If we are truly living a Christ-centered life, we should praise God in the good times and the bad times. Often, we want to take credit for the good times, and God gets to take all the blame for anything negative that happens. By offering up praise immediately after a sale, we can assume an attitude of gratitude and replace self for thankfulness. Offering up our praise and acknowledging God for the blessing helps us put the focus squarely on Christ. Proverbs 3:5–6 says we should trust in the Lord with all our heart and lean not on our own. In all our ways, we should acknowledge Him and God will make our path straight.

So the next time you close a sale, go into your happy dance, sing your song at full volume and offer up the praise to the Lord for what He has done! I think by doing this, you'll see "self" disappear in the rearview mirror and be replaced by a heart of thankfulness.

Have you experienced any recent success that perhaps you've failed to acknowledge God for the blessing? Take a few minutes and think through some recent sales, and give God the glory!

....

> Jesus, thank You for the business You have brought to me. You are a faithful provider. I acknowledge that every good and perfect gift is from You. Any credit that I may try to take is simply utilizing skills and gifts that You have blessed me with. I honor You by giving You all the praise! Thank You, Jesus! Amen!

ASK, SEEK, AND KNOCK

> Ask and it will be given to you; seek and you will find; knock and the door will be opened to you. For everyone who asks receives; the one who seeks finds; and to the one who knocks, the door will be opened.
> —Matthew 7:7

We live in a time of a "name it and claim it" type of religion. We often think of Jesus as the genie in the magic bottle. Matthew 7 says to "ask and it will be given," but often, we want to stop right there. The rest of the verse says we are to seek and to knock. These are words that require action. In our sales role, yes, we are to ask God; but we have a responsibility to seek and to knock. We need to seek new customers, we should seek opportunities, and we are to be knocking on our clients' doors. Quite often, we put God in a difficult spot. We want his blessings, but we are not living up to our responsibilities to be a person of action.

Perhaps we have gotten lazy in our sales activities. We're relying on yesterday's efforts and not setting new strategies for today. I think in every sales role there are peaks and valleys. There are times if we're being honest that we put forth more effort and other times that we take a timeout. We have to be true and honest with ourselves and really do a hard evaluation on our own personal efforts. Are we guilty of asking God to provide but we are not seeking and knocking in our own efforts? Maybe today is a good day to be honest with ourselves, do a self-evaluation and determine if our daily activities are leading to action.

What activities can I do today to recalibrate my strategies?

Lord, I know that my efforts are sometimes lacking. I'm guilty of expecting You to provide and to bless my work, and I'm not putting forth the best effort each day. Help me to be honest with myself. Provide new motivation. Give me a renewed sense of purpose and direction in my job. God, thank You that if we ask, You will indeed provide. Thank You for showing me that I need not only to ask but also to seek and to knock as well. Thank You in Jesus's name! Amen!

COLLABORATION

> Some men took a man who was not able to move his body to Jesus. He was carried on a bed. But they could not find a way to take him in because of so many people. They made a hole in the roof over where Jesus stood. Then they let the bed with the sick man on it down before Jesus. When Jesus saw their faith, He said to the man, "Friend, your sins are forgiven." At once the sick man got up in front of them. He took his bed and went to his home thanking God.
> —Luke 5:18–20, 25

In every sales role, you will face obstacles. Perhaps your competition is less expensive, existing client relationships with other providers, your product doesn't perform exactly as the customer expects, you don't offer the right color choice, the item may not fit their budget, you don't have the item in stock, or the product is obsolete. There can be a whole host of reasons why a customer may decide to not purchase your item or prevent you from making the sale. Luke tells a story of a man that was so sick, injured or crippled that he couldn't even walk. Whatever the case, he was bed-stricken and couldn't walk. The story says the crowds were also so big he couldn't come through the front door to where Jesus was standing. His friends would not be deterred. They carried the man up to the roof, cut a hole in the ceiling, and lowered him down; and the Bible says he was healed. This required out-of-the-box thinking, a creative solution, strategy, and collaboration with friends.

Perhaps you are in an industry or sell a product that has enormous obstacles. Maybe you have a difficult prospect and just can't figure out how to get close enough to them in order to be heard? Just like the man that was so sick he couldn't walk, can you develop a new strategy to make progress and move the potential sale along?

Start thinking, "Who do I know that can help me, or is there another way into this potential sale?" This may require collaboration with a coworker, someone that knows the client or another sales representative that is in a complimentary role. It may require asking for help internally with other resources. Just like this man, he had to rely on some friends to carry him to the roof and lower him down. Think through your strategies and a fresh new approach to the client.

What obstacles are you facing? Make a list of what you're trying to accomplish with each sale, the challenges you face with this prospect, and think through who you can collaborate with or another way you can gain access to this client.

> Jesus, thank You for being a Savior that has given me a creative mind and able to think of new strategies. Help me open new doors, see new opportunities, and find new ways in the door. I praise You for being a Savior that cares about my sales. Thank You for loving me and opening up new opportunities. I give You all the praise and glory, for it's only through Your name I pray! Amen!

LOOK AT THE HEART

> But the Lord said to Samuel, "Do not look on his appearance or on the height of his stature, because I have rejected him. For the Lord sees not as man sees: man looks on the outward appearance, but the Lord looks on the heart."
> —1 Samuel 16:7

Do not judge someone based on their appearance. This is a simple principle that applies to not only to a sales position but to every aspect of your life. This lesson was once reaffirmed to me when I worked in sales at a marine dealership. It was a cold, slow day at the marina. Not the ideal weather for selling a boat. As several of us was gathered around chatting as often happened on slow days, in walks a group of four guys. All of them dressed like they're looking for a barn to clean out. I tell the other salespersons that I would "go run them off." Well, it ended up being one of the most famous drivers in NASCAR. None of us had recognized him. He had enough money to buy the entire dealership, let alone a boat if he wanted to. The story ends with him, buying one of our most expensive boats without even negotiating for a deep discount. Lesson learned!

We have all heard stories of CEOs, wealthy individuals, trust-fund families, or someone that we stereotyped and didn't fit "our" model of what a customer should look like get ignored when they were trying to buy something just because of their appearance. By the same token, I've heard numerous stories of individuals that at first appearance you would think could buy anything only to find out their credit is so poor they can't even afford to buy a cup of coffee on credit. They're all show without any real financial substance. Well, the lesson is obvious here: Treat each opportunity, prospective customers, individuals with respect and dignity. Assume they can afford to buy anything you are selling. It's often very tempting to try to hunt down the "elephant" account or chase the biggest brand-name prospect when in fact, you may have a better opportunity that can afford what you're selling and become a loyal customer of yours for years.

Review your prospect list. Are there potential clients that you have ignored because they don't "appear" to be the model customer? Are there changes in your stereotypes and opinions that need to be made?

> Gracious heavenly Father, help me to have discernment. Thank You for reminding me to always look at the heart of a person and not the outward appearance. Forgive me where I've treated someone wrong based on opinions I've formed. Help me to open my eyes, my heart, and my ears to hear, see, and learn from You. In Jesus's name I pray! Amen!

SHREWD AS A SERPENT

> Behold, I am sending you out as a sheep in the midst of wolves, so be wise as serpents and innocent as doves.
> —Matthew 10:16

In Matthew 10, Jesus is giving his disciples instructions and letting them know that persecution will come as a follower of Christ. He is letting them know as they go out into the world, they will face hard times and challenging situations. He tells them to be wise as serpents. Some translations say to be shrewd as a snake. Being shrewd is defined as having or showing sharp powers of judgment, being astute. As a sales professional, we must possess great judgment. You must be able to think strategically and be relentless and determined in our pursuit of an opportunity. Being shrewd does not mean to be dishonest.

Jesus also tells them to be innocent as doves. Is it possible to be shrewd and innocent at the same time? To be innocent does not mean to be passive or soft. To be innocent is to be blameless, honest, transparent, and ethical. In our sales profession, we do not want to be deceitful, cunning, scheming, or unethical. We can all get caught up in the emotion of chasing that big deal, rising to the challenge of closing the next sale or feel the mounting pressure of a quota. In Matthew 10:19, Jesus goes on to tell his disciples that when they feel the persecution coming not to be anxious or show fear, the spirit will lead them, guide them, and speak through them. As you are out in the marketplace, the temptation may come that you have create a devious plan in order to succeed. Do not give into that thought. Be as Jesus said, shrewd as a serpent but always be innocent as a dove!

Have you found yourself tempted to be deceitful? Think through those areas where you may have compromised your values and as God to help you be bold!

> Jesus, I come before You and acknowledge that I haven't always operated with integrity. I ask You to forgive me when I have misled or been deceitful to others. Thank You for showing me that I can be shrewd in business and be completely innocent and blameless before You. Thank You, Father! In the name of Jesus I pray! Amen!

HOPE IS A STRATEGY

> But in your hearts honor Christ the Lord as holy, always being prepared to make a defense to anyone who asks you for a reason for the hope that is in you; yet do it with gentleness and respect,
> —1 Peter 3:15

Vince Lombardi has been credited with saying, "Hope is not a strategy. Fear is not an option." This phrase has even been used as the title for a sales help book. I would agree; there's no substitute for a well-thought-out and executed business plan. I would suggest, however, as a Christian, our hope in Christ is not only a good idea, it is the *only* strategy. Hope is a strategy. Psalm 20:7 says, "Some trusts in chariots and some in horses but we trust in the name of the Lord our God." We are all guilty at times of placing more trust and hope in our "things" or our "material possessions" than we do in the Lord. We have the arrogance to think that we have accomplished our success on our own without ever giving the credit or glory to God. We may trust in our own intellect, we trust our partners, we place trust in our company to carry out plans, and we falsely put our trust in a variety of areas. As a Christian in the workplace, our customers, our coworkers, or business partners should be able to see a difference in us. They should see a difference in the way we conduct our business, the way we respond to a victory or defeat. They should see that we place our hope in something beyond our sales. We should be prepared to give an answer for this reason for hope. What does this mean? When we have success, we give credit to God. When we have a failure, we don't blame God. When something turns unexpectedly, they should see us respond differently. When we have conflict with customers or with coworkers, we should react different than expected. When conflict does occur, we should be quick to work for reconciliation. When our customers, partners, coworkers see us respond different than the way the world would respond, it may just open the door to tell them the reason for our hope! Hope is a strategy!

Are there areas in your daily business that doesn't accurately reflect our hope we have in Christ? Are there times that you have not conducted yourself in a Christ-like manner? Is there anyone you need to repair a damaged relationship with?

....

> Lord, thank You for being my Hope! You are my hope, and it's in You I place my trust. Any success that I have is only through Your gracious blessings. Thank You for being concerned about every aspect of my life! I ask You to give me strength to conduct myself in my daily business with kindness and respect for others! Amen!

SPIRITUAL MARKERS

> When the whole nation had finished crossing the Jordan, the LORD said to Joshua, "Choose twelve men from among the people, one from each tribe, and tell them to take up twelve stones from the middle of the Jordan, from right where the priests are standing, and carry them over with you and put them down at the place where you stay tonight."
> —Joshua 4:1–3

Spiritual memory is vital to the Christian life. You will experience times throughout your sales career when you just don't know how God is going to pull you through. It is important to remember times when you have called upon the Lord, He has answered prayers and God has been faithful.

God instructed Joshua to select stones from the middle of the Jordan River where they had just crossed on dry ground. It was a time for them where everything seemed hopeless; they had run into a dead end, but God showed his faithfulness allowing the Israelites to cross right through the middle of the river. Never even getting one drop of water on them. The twelve stones represented each tribe and was to be laid as a marker to remember this occasion. They were to mark this moment and recall God's faithfulness the next time everything seemed impossible.

Having spiritual markers from a time when you clearly experienced God's mercy and His deliverance is important to reflect on when times seems bleak. It is vital to be able to recall how God pulled you through. I have a friend that has a very successful expedited freight business. He often tells stories of when he was a young newlywed, and to say they didn't have much would be a major understatement. He vividly recalls times they chose to give their tithe, and they didn't know where rent money was going to come from. Each and every time, he says God was faithful and never let them get behind on rent and always had food to eat. God would bring a customer in, and unexpectedly, he would make a sale right when they needed it most. Now some thirty years later and with a successful business, he still recalls with excitement those memories of God's faithfulness. Those are spiritual markers in his life. There's a saying that says, "God is never early, but he's always right on time."

Can you recall any specific times in your life when you clearly saw God's faithful hand? Reflect back on those times and make a spiritual marker on the occasion.

....

> God, You are a mighty and a strong tower in my life. Thank You for your faithfulness. Thank You for every time You have come through for me. Help me to recall those times, and I offer them up as a praise offering to You! Amen!

RUN THE RACE

> Do you not know that in a race all runners run, but only one receives the prize? So run that you may obtain it.
> —1 Corinthians 9:24

There was a popular comedy movie about a race car driver and the motto of the leading character was, "If you're not first, you're last." This statement could not be more true than in a sales role. Second place never pays in a sales deal. There is no prize for second place. Nothing is more frustrating than to find out you was the customer's second choice. It may even hurt more when you run into an old prospect only to have them say, "I should have bought it from you!" You're like, "Thanks, appreciate that!" A little too late now!

First Corinthians 9:24 has been a favorite verse of mine since I was a kid. I was always very competitive in athletics. I liked to win and probably hated losing even more. I like the way the KJV translates this verse: "Know ye not that they which run in a race run all, but one receiveth the prize? So run, that ye may obtain." That gets me fired up and going just reading those words. "Run that ye may obtain." The first time I read this verse, I said, "There it is right there in the Bible. You must run to win!" It seemed to justify my competitive nature. In our sales role, second place doesn't pay. We must as we are doing our job compete to win. It is first place or nothing. It's not first place at any cost, but we must strive to win if we are doing our job.

I have since come to know this verse is not just referring to a sports competition or even a sale, but it's referring to the greatest race of all, the race we are running in life. The prize that we should strive to obtain is not a temporary trophy or award, but the crown offered only by a surrendered Christ-centered life. Verse 25 says, "Athletes train to get a crown that will not last but we do it to get a crown that will last forever." Just as we must train for a sports competition, we must keep sharp in our sales profession as well. We must also keep sharp in our Christian walk. How do we do that? We do that by maintaining a consistent prayer life and keeping in God's word. We do this by living out a surrendered life to Christ.

In your race, are you staying sharp? Do you still approach your job with the passion? Are you in strict training just like an Olympic athlete would?

> Dear heavenly Father, thank You for giving me a competitive spirit. Help me to run a race that is pleasing to You. Thank You for providing for me and helping me. In Jesus's name I pray! Amen!

HUMILITY

> Do nothing from selfish ambition or conceit, but in humility count others more significant than yourselves. Let each of you look not only to his own interests, but also to the interests of others.
> —Philippians 2:3–4

We live in a time that self-centeredness seems to be a rite of passage. It's all about me. You don't have to look for an example of self-indulgence any further than at the local coffee shop. Just sit and listen to most of the orders that come through and you'll hear the "me" attitude. "I'll have a half caff, grande latte, extra frothy foam served at room temperature only, make sure it is hand-stirred, white granular organic sugar, stir in the cream with a petrified forest wooden spoon, almond milk from almonds grown in the Himalayans only, no MSG, make sure it's gluten free, and serve it at ninety-seven degrees. Don't put the lid on until the steam has simmered." Come on, please; you can almost hear the self-indulgence ooze in the order. How about this: Just a cup of coffee please? Hey, I'm not knocking the cultured pallet of a trained coffee connoisseur. I'm merely saying that most of us have an attitude that "I deserve this" or "I have earned that." I'm more important than you! Most of us have the attitude that we are the humblest person I know. Listen, there is nothing wrong with a latte, but the point I am making is consider our motives and what's in our heart when we do anything.

Philippians says that we should do nothing from our own selfish ambition, but we should consider others more highly than ourselves. How do we do consider others in our sales role when, after all, if we don't make the sale, we may actually suffer? It starts with our attitude. Do we have a gracious attitude and operate with a spirit of humility, or do we have a take no prisoners and step on anyone in the way just to make the sale attitude? As a sales rep, it is our job to win it is our job to close the sale, but we can operate with an attitude of thankfulness and humility in doing our job. It starts with acknowledging God in all that we do. Christ set the example for us by lowering himself and taking the form of a servant. We acknowledge that through Christ Jesus, He has blessed you with the job, the mind to perform your sales role, He's placed customers in your path, He has given you ideas and strategies to help position your sales role. We have an attitude of humility when interacting with our coworkers, support staff, our sales partners. We can be successful while maintaining an attitude of gratefulness.

Do you see examples of a lack of humility in your own life? Take a second and think through some areas where you have maybe put yourself before others?

> Lord, I confess that I don't always have an attitude of humility. I acknowledge that everything I do and have is only because of You. Forgive me for falling short. Help lead and guide me this day to consider others. Thank You, Jesus! Amen!

QUICK TO LISTEN

> My dear brothers and sisters, take note of
> this. Everyone should be quick to listen, slow
> to speak and slow to become angry.
>
> —James 1:19

I have heard it said before that God gave us two ears and only one mouth for a reason. We should do more listening than talking. I know as a sales rep, keeping our mouth shut and letting someone else do the talking can be painful. After all, we like to spew out advice, share our opinions, and we like to be heard. There's a sales principle that says whoever does the most talking goes home with the product. In other words, if you as a sales rep and do all the talking, chances are, you're not making the sale. We've all heard various terms referring to sales philosophies: needs-based sales, solution selling, consultative selling approach, relationship selling, SPIN approach, conceptual selling, SNAP approach, the challenger sale, Sandler methodology, and countless others. The one thing that all sales techniques, methodologies, systems, or approaches have in common is you have to get the customer talking. You have to uncover their needs, find out their pain points, their objections, and their interests. You have to build rapport and trust. In order to do this, you have to have dialogue, and in order to build this trust, you have to listen to the customer's needs, wants, desires, and challenges. You have to listen.

James 1:19 says we should be quick to listen and slow to speak. In this simple verse, the writer states the most basic sales principle: Let the customer do the talking. Everyone likes to be the expert and likes to be heard. Slow down, take a deep breath, and take an interest in your customer. Let the customer be heard. We should be applying this same principle in our prayer life. Slow down, take a deep breath, and listen to God. Be slow to speak and quick to listen!

Can you make a conscientious effort today to slow down and let your customers be heard? Can you take a deep breath and listen for God's voice in your life?

....

> Gracious Lord and Savior, I bow humbly before You and ask for You to help me to be slow to speak and quick to listen. Let me hear Your voice today! Let me listen for instructions from you. Help me to apply this in my job. Help me to take an interest in my customers and consider their needs before my own. In Jesus's name! Amen!

DO NOT BE DISMAYED

So do not fear, for I am with you; do not be dismayed,
for I am your God. I will strengthen you and help you;
I will uphold you with my righteous right hand.
—Isaiah 41:10

I have experienced times in my sales life where I completely feel dismayed. What does it mean to be dismayed to begin with? To lose courage or to be upset or perturbed. *Perturbed*, now that's a good word. That word seems to fit those times when you just feel like giving up. Those times when you feel like the "sales prevention department" is doing everything to work against you. You know that department. Most companies have one. They're supposed to be the sales support staff, but they seem to do everything they can to try and work against you closing a deal or supporting the client. You worked tirelessly on closing a deal just to have the finance department cut them off or deny their credit. You get the order and the shipping department botched up the freight and can't get the materials out on time. Customer service seems to be doing everything they can to upset your customer. Someone decides to cut travel costs when your best customer has a crisis and needs to see you and you have to tell them travel has been denied. These are times of just feeling perturbed at the situation. I've even had experiences where I feel like it's time to move on, you interview somewhere, you get your hopes up only to be told they're going with a different candidate. God just seems to be closing all the doors. If you're really being honest, you may even be saying, "God, where are you? I'm struggling down here!"

What do you do in these times? Isaiah says, "Do not fear, Do not be dismayed—God will strengthen you." In these situations, you have to hit the pause button, get real with God, and lay it out that you're struggling. Let God know, "This doesn't make sense, and I don't think I'm hearing from You, but Your word says that You will hold me up with your righteous hand! I am trusting You to strengthen me and to help me!" Do not be dismayed!

Are you experiencing a time that you feel perturbed? Be honest with God and let Him know where you're struggling. Are you having a good season right now? Capture these times so you can remember them later.

> God, I come humbly before You and confess, I don't "feel" You right now. I trust Your word that You will strengthen me. I ask for that strength now. I ask You to uphold me with Your righteousness. I ask You to make my paths straight. Give me a new outlook and a new attitude. Let me see Your mighty hand at work. I love You, and I praise You. Amen!

PREPARATION

"There is a boy here who has five barley loaves and two fish, but what are they for so many?" Jesus then took the loaves, and when he had given thanks, he distributed them to those who were seated. So also the fish, as much as they wanted.
—John 6:9, 11

There are two accounts of Jesus feeding the multitude using bread and fish. Each of the Gospels records the feeding of five thousand, and Matthew and Mark record the feeding of four thousand. Most people focus on the miracle of Jesus feeding so many with so little. True, this is an absolute miracle and a beautiful example of Jesus meeting the very basic needs of the people by providing food. Only John mentions the little boy that brought food that day. Over five thousand people came to hear and see Jesus on this day, yet the Bible only mentions this little boy as being the only one that planned ahead. Perhaps he had a caring mother that packed his lunch that morning, or maybe he knew he would be gone all day and brought his lunch? Regardless, the boy was prepared. He knew it was going to be a long day, and he would get hungry.

I have two sons of my own, and my wife is relentless about packing a snack for them, especially when they were younger. I don't think we could drive across town without a snack of some kind being packed in the car. My wife has discovered that proper planning makes for a much happier trip. The same can be said about sales. Making the proper preparations is vital for success in sales. If we are being honest, how much planning do we put in before our sales calls? I know I have been guilty of scheduling a meeting and not putting a thought into the call until I pull into the clients parking lot. How do you think those meetings turn out? Just like this boy, we can separate ourselves out from the rest of the mob by putting the proper amount of preparation in for our sales meetings. This means conducting proper prospecting, research, analysis, gaining knowledge about your own products, and your prospective client. You should be making the proper preparations before your meetings both with information and mentally. It has been said that for every minute in a meeting, at least double the time should be devoted to preparing for the meeting.

President Franklin Roosevelt once said, "By failing to prepare you are preparing to fail." Preparation requires effort, but the reward can be great.

How would you rate your preparation for your sales calls or meetings? What are some things that you could do to help you be better prepared to do your job?

....

>   Lord, thank You for providing for me. Thank You for teaching me lessons on being prepared. Help me and show me where I need to make better preparations this day! In Jesus's name I pray! Amen!

PROFITABLE FOR TEACHING

> All Scripture is breathed out by God and profitable
> for teaching, for reproof, for correction, and for
> training in righteousness, that the man of God may
> be complete, equipped for every good work.
> —2 Timothy 3:16–17

Do you think of the Bible as a sales instruction book? Does it serve as a guide that can help show you and point you in the right direction for your sales career? I am guilty of wanting to compartmentalize God. I say I want His help in every area of my life, but in reality, I only want His input in when I'm in a real battle. Often my thoughts are "You can have control over here but not in this part of my life." "Help me with my kids and my family, but when it comes to my business, I'll take care of that." A recurring theme is "My sales numbers are down, so now, God, you can jump in and bail me out." Often never considering what God's word says on a daily basis for guidance in my sales activities.

Second Timothy 3 says that all scripture is breathed by God and is profitable for teaching and for training. If the Bible was given to us for teaching and training, then it was given to us for every aspect of our life. This includes your sales life as well. It was given to us and can serve as a roadmap for our job in sales. Hidden within the verses are applications that not only apply to daily living but for our daily sales activities as well. Psalm 119:105 says, "Thy word is a lamp unto my feet, and a light unto my path." The Bible was given to us as a guide for our entire life. As you read through the Bible, start looking for the specific applications for your sales career. We can begin to incorporate God's principles in every aspect of our life, including your sales. What we're really talking about is Lordship. By applying all of God's principles contained in His word, we are able to make Christ Lord of our life!

Have you considered God's word as the ultimate guide for your entire life, including your sales activities? How can you begin to do this today?

> Thank You, Lord, for giving us your Word. I acknowledge that Your Word, the Bible, was given to us as a gift to help guide me through my life. Help me to see your applications and apply the principles to every aspect of my life, including my job. Thank You for caring about every detail of my life! I love You, Lord! Amen!

KNOWLEDGE

*An intelligent heart acquires knowledge, and
the ear of the wise seeks knowledge.*
—Proverbs 18:15

Socrates was quoted as saying, "The only true wisdom is in knowing you know nothing." The moment we begin to think that we know everything about sales that we will ever need to know is the moment that you will fail. Knowledge is the key that unlocks the door to opportunities. Knowledge is the foundation that we build our sales success upon. We should strive to become the industry expert in your chosen field. Think of it as developing your own personal brand within your marketplace. Just think, if we learned just one new thing every day, how much more would you know at the end of this year alone?

Proverbs tells us that an intelligent heart acquires knowledge. We should strive to learn as much as we possibly can about our products, services, and our offering. We should never stop developing our selling techniques, learning new systems or gaining a deeper understanding of our offering. We should continue to develop ourselves personally and professionally. Continue to educate ourselves on the latest trends, technologies, and products within our given sales field. The more we know, the more we will grow. If we are not growing, then we are dying. So continue to grow!

Are there areas where you need to gain more knowledge? What can you do today to continue the learning and growing process?

Lord, thank You for giving me a mind that can learn and understand. I acknowledge that true wisdom comes from knowing You and You alone.

In my job, help me to continue to grow, learn, and apply what I've learned. Thank You and in Jesus's name I pray! Amen!

ASK FOR WISDOM

> If any of you lacks wisdom, let him ask God, who gives generously to all without reproach, and it will be given to him. But let him ask in faith, with no doubting, for the one who doubts is like a wave of the sea that is driven and tossed by the wind.
> —James 1:5–6

What is the difference between wisdom and knowledge? Both recurring Bible themes are related, but they are not the same. Knowledge is really about facts and ideas that we acquire through study, research, investigation and observation. Wisdom, on the other hand, is the ability to discern and judge those aspects of knowledge that are true, right, lasting, and has application to your life. Knowledge can exist without wisdom but not the other way around. One can be knowledgeable without being wise. It has been said that knowledge speaks, but wisdom listens. Albert Einstein said, "Any fool can know. The point is to understand." To understand is to have wisdom.

Proverbs says, "The fear of the Lord is the beginning of knowledge, but fools despise wisdom and knowledge." Our foundation for knowledge must begin with our relationship with Jesus Christ. Making Christ Lord of our life is the starting line for our path to any knowledge and wisdom. In our sales role, it is vital to have knowledge. We should strive to gain as much knowledge, insight, and information as possible. Having this information will only better position you for future success. Having knowledge without wisdom is the same as knowing how to build a bicycle without knowing how to ride it. James says that if we lack wisdom, we should ask God for it, and as his children, He will give it generously. Gain all the knowledge you can, but ask God for wisdom in how to apply it to help make us more prosperous in our roles.

Is Christ Lord of your life? Have you asked God to provide you wisdom for doing your job?

> Lord Jesus, Your word says You will provide wisdom generously if we just ask. I come humbly before You now asking You to provide wisdom to help me with my sales role. Show me how to apply the knowledge that I've gained. Help me in every area of my life! In Jesus's name I pray! Amen!

REASON FOR OUR HOPE

> But in your hearts revere Christ as Lord. Always be prepared to give an answer to everyone who asks you to give the reason for the hope that you have. But do this with gentleness and respect.
> —1 Peter 3:15

    I recently had a conversation with a friend of mine, and I told him that if my life was an advertisement for Christian living, it probably would not attract very many customers. It is a sad commentary for the Christian life on the example that I often set with my attitude. I know of an atheist who refuses to believe there is a God but displays more joy than I often do. Jeremiah 29 says that Lord declares the plans for us. Plans not to harm us but plans to give us hope and a future. As a Christ follower, our coworkers, customers, friends, and neighbors should see a difference. They should be curious where our hope comes from. How do we show others where our hope comes from in our marketplace? We can start by not complaining. Philippians says to do all things without grumbling and complaining. That's a good place to start!

    A company that I worked for once hired a former motivational speaker and life coach to join the team. His message was that we should all have optimism and if we believe it, the universe will manifest it into existence. There was no mention of God only some invisible cosmic force that by some chance makes things happen. In Romans 8, it says that God causes all things to work for good for those who love God. We who revere Christ as Lord know where our true hope comes from. First Peter says we should always be prepared to tell others the reason for this hope. But we need to do it with gentleness and respect. So today, display the hope that Christ promises us.

Does your life reflect the hope in Jesus Christ that he promises us? What can you do today to make the changes in your attitude that will better reflect Christ's love?

....

> Jesus, You are my reason for hope! Help me to do all things without grumbling and complaining. Let me be prepared to give a reason for my hope! Thank You for loving me and thank You for saving me! In Jesus's name I pray! Amen!

FEAR NOT

> Then he said to me, Fear not, Daniel, for from the first day that you set your heart to understand and humbled yourself before God, your words have been heard, and I have come because of your words.
> —Daniel 10:12

Is there a client, coworker, account, friend, neighbor, or some other situation that you have been praying for; and you just don't seem to be hearing from God or getting an answer? Maybe you're praying for a new job, praying for success in your current role, perhaps there's a big account that you've been praying to close for a long time? Perhaps you've been praying for new direction or purpose in your life, but the answers just aren't coming. In Daniel 10:12, the verse says that Daniel also had been praying but help wasn't coming. It says he had been praying and had set his heart on understanding, but the answer just wasn't showing up. In verse 13, it explains that for twenty-one days, the angel had been delayed. The angel had been caught up in battling spiritual warfare for twenty-one days and not until the archangel Michael came to help were they victorious and able to come and deliver the news and answer Daniel's prayer.

We can have confidence that from the first moment we pray and humble ourselves before God, that He has heard that prayer, and it is already answered. True faith comes in believing during the quite times. I find the silent moments when nothing seems to be happening, an answer just isn't coming, and no help seems to be in sight is the most difficult to truly trust and have faith. This lesson in Daniel provides hope that God is working on our behalf. Our job is to keep praying. From the first day that Daniel had humbled himself before the Lord, his prayer had been heard. We can have confidence in knowing that just like Daniel, from the first day we set our heart on God, that our prayer has been heard and our prayer is answered!

What have you been praying for that you don't feel like God is hearing? Take a moment and lay that before the Lord. Now, have confidence that your prayer has been heard and God has already answered it!

> Lord, I must confess that often in the silent times is when fear sets in, I lose confidence, and my faith in You is tested! Thank You for being a powerful God that loves me in spite of my fear! Set my heart on trusting You! Let me have confidence that You have heard my prayer, and I can rest assured You are working, and it is answered! Thank You in Jesus's name! Amen!

EMBRACE THE PAUSE

> This they said to test him, that they might have some charge to bring against him. Jesus bent down and wrote with his finger in the ground. And as they continued to ask him, he stood up and said to them, "Let him who is without sin among you be the first to throw a stone at her."
> —John 8:6–7

As a sales rep, we often feel compelled to make sure there's not a single moment of silence in a sales call. One single second of no one talking can feel like an eternity. Radio personalities call this "dead air." Dead air in a sales call or presentation makes us feel uncomfortable, doesn't it? We feel pressured to have the perfect answer on the tip of our tongue for any given situation. As a seasoned sales veteran, we need to train ourselves to appreciate the pause. If a customer asks a direct question, there is nothing wrong with taking a few seconds to gather your thoughts and prepare a well-thought-out answer before speaking.

In John 8, the Pharisees was trying to trick Jesus by asking him what they felt were some tough, direct questions. Instead of "taking the bait," Jesus simply paused, bent down, and started writing in the sand. Jesus didn't immediately start get defensive, start defending himself, try to justify an answer, or develop some colorful story response. He simply listened as the Pharisees spoke and before he answered, he paused and gathered his thoughts. What you will notice, however, in the verse is when Jesus did speak, He stood up; no doubt looked them in the eye; and asked a very direct, thought-out, and well-articulated challenging question. And when they heard the question, verse 9 says they one by one began to leave. That's the power of the pause. It allows you to gather your thoughts and develop a clear and concise response. There's power in the pause! Think about that. Let the customer do the talking, and don't be afraid of a pause in the conversation so each of you can gather your thoughts. It will send a signal to the customer that you're not just making up answers, but you're serious and extremely thoughtful in your response. So on your next sales call, don't be afraid of dead air. Embrace the pause!

Are you guilty of trying to have the perfect answer for every possible question? Does the pause in a presentation make you feel uncomfortable? In your next sales presentation, remind yourself that it's okay to take a second to gather your thoughts.

....

> Jesus, thank You for the lessons You teach us. Your word was given for instruction in every aspect of my life. Thank You for showing us that we should be slow to speak and quick to listen. Help me to embrace the pause in my work, with my family, and in my life! Thank You, Jesus! Amen!

SPEAK WITH KINDNESS

> Let your speech always be with grace, seasoned with salt,
> that you may know how you ought to answer each one.
> —Colossians 4:6

It often feels like we live in a time where people think they have the right to speak to anyone in any way they feel. We think we can speak our mind, and who cares if we offend anyone. Colossians 4:6 says our speech should always be filled with grace.

I remember standing in line one time at a grocery store. And as it often happens at a grocery store, an item was missing the price, requiring the cashier to call for a price check. Well, of course, this slows the line down, and it starts backing up for what felt like an eternity. Standing further back in the line, this person who happened to be a medical doctor was standing with his ten-year-old son. He blurts out this obscenity directed at this young, high-school-age cashier, sending her into tears. I understand the frustration as we all felt the frustration, but the anger he showed and the speech he used was totally uncalled for. What a message to send to his ten-year-old son that we are more important than her, and we have the right to speak to her any way we want. What a sad example he set that day.

In the sales role that you are in, customers can often think they have the right to speak to you any way they want since, after all, they are the customers. As a sales rep, we need to rise above this, and when we speak, choose to let our speech be filled with grace and seasoned with salt. Salt tenderizes the meat and acts as a preservative, keeping food fresh, allowing it to be stored for longer time. That's the way our speech should be to others. It should season the conversation and be uplifting to others. Our speech should act as a preservative to the other person. That is the example we want to set to our customers, our friends, and our families!

Have you allowed your speech with others to become unpleasant? Do you ever join in on conversations that are not uplifting? Have you ever had a meeting where words were spoken that did not bring glory to the Lord? Ask for God to help you with your speech today!

> Lord, most gracious heavenly Father. Forgive me where I've used speech that was unwholesome and did not glorify Your name. Help me to view others more highly than myself. Let me use my words to be edifying and uplifting to others. Grant me wisdom in my daily conversations. Let my words be filled with grace! In Jesus's name I pray! Amen!

SIMPLE OBEDIENCE

> Then the Lord said, "As my servant Isaiah has walked naked and barefoot for three years as a sign and a portent against Egypt and Cush."
> —Isaiah 20:3

There are a lot of stories in the Bible that I quite frankly don't understand. Isaiah 20 tells of a story where God commands Isaiah to take off his clothes and walk naked for three years. Can you imagine what everyone in the neighborhood must have thought? "Hey, kids, here comes naked Isaiah again, run in the house!" What a sight this must have been. I'm sure for Isaiah it was God: "You want me to do what?" It probably didn't make sense to Isaiah as well, but he had seen God's faithfulness and simply followed in obedience. As the story unfolds, you see that God had a purpose in asking Isaiah to walk naked. It would be a sign against Egypt and Cush.

If I'm being honest, sometimes, God may say to do something that just doesn't make sense to you and me, but God has a purpose in everything he does. We can take confidence in knowing that God's plans are perfect. Jeremiah 29:11 says that God has a plan for us. His plans are to prosper us and not harm us. We have a hope and a future in Christ Jesus. We have this promise. I have heard it said that delayed obedience is disobedience. Is there something that God has laid on your heart that just doesn't make sense, and you have failed to follow his instructions? Ask God to make it clear what He wants you to do. Maybe it's to go back to a customer that you had a terrible experience with, and it may be completely embarrassing, but God has a plan with them? Maybe there's a coworker, friend, or neighbor that you need to ask for help, and your pride is not allowing that. Is it a job change, difficult task at work, fear of public speaking, or something else? Listen to God for his instructions and simply be obedient.

Has God been instructing you to do something that you don't think makes sense?

....

> My heavenly Father, sometimes if I'm being honest, I simply don't understand the plans that You have for me. I want to know all the details before I step out and follow. I confess that my doubt is really fear. I ask for Your help to give me strength to simply obey. Give me courage to trust You no matter what You ask. Help me to know that You have a purpose in everything You do. Help me to grow closer to You. In Jesus's name I pray! Amen!

KEYS TO HAPPINESS

> Our mouths were filled with laughter, our tongues with songs of joy. Then it was said among the nations, "The Lord has done great things for them." The Lord has done great things for us, and we are filled with joy.
> —Psalm 126:2–3

As a professional sales representative, it is extremely difficult to remain in a constant state of gratitude. After all, for most sales roles, you're dealing with more loss than wins. Even the best closing ratio is never going to be 100 percent An optimistic outlook is contagious. If we are filled with laughter and joy, then others will look at what great things the Lord has done, and they will be filled with joy as well. You know that you're more effective when you're in that "happy" place in your mind. Your enthusiasm is inspiring and you're much more productive when you're in a good place.

So what are some keys to happiness? Of course it starts with our relationship with the Lord. Can you confidently say that Jesus Christ is Lord of your life? Let me also suggest six ways to remain happy.

1. *Physical movement.* Try to do some kind of physical activity every day.
2. *Remain in a state of gratitude.* Be grateful. Gratitude impacts your attitude.
3. *Opportunities.* Have a mindset this is being done *for me* not *to me*!
4. *Daily prayer.* Be in a constant state of prayer.
5. *Random acts of kindness.* Look for ways to help others.
6. *Reflect on what is going well.* Ask yourself, what went well today?

As Psalm 126 says, "Let our mouths be filled with laughter and our tongues with songs of joy." Laugh today! Crank the music up and sign out loud today. Smile. If you don't feel like smiling, then fake it till you make it. The Lord has done great things for us; let us be glad!

Is Jesus Christ Lord of your life? If not, ask him now to come into your life, and be Lord of your life. Reflect on the six suggestions for happiness and see if there's any areas that you can improve?

....

> Lord, thank You for all that You have done. I confess that I am not always grateful, and I do not always acknowledge Your presence in my life. Help me today to be more grateful. Let me be aware of others and help me to reflect on Your goodness. In Jesus's name I pray! Amen!

PHYSICAL MOVEMENT

> Beloved, I pray that all may go well with you and that you may be in good health, as it goes well with your soul.
> —3 John 1:2

Sales can be a difficult profession to maintain a healthy lifestyle, especially if you travel extensively for your job. Staying in hotels, eating out, and entertaining clients, grabbing a quick meal at the fast-food drive through or just working long hours can make for a challenge to maintain good choices. It can be hard to stay active. Third John says that it goes well with your soul to be in good health. Some type of daily activity can help improve your mood, boost your energy, prevent excess weight gain, promote better sleep, and just improve your overall outlook. Daily movement helps get the blood moving and helps to get your brain in gear and ready to sell.

You may not be a world-class athlete or able to run a marathon, but you can still have some type of physical movement. Start your day off by doing some jumping jacks or taking a walk, take a break from your day, and do a push-up or stretch. Anything you can do to help introduce physical activity into your daily routine may help improve your overall outlook. As we all know, if you're active and feeling good, it will make you more productive. The more productive you are, the better your chances of closing more deals.

Incorporating exercise into your daily routine will help, but that alone will not improve your attitude. We should also try to monitor our diet. Improved eating habits go along with physical movement. "You are what you eat" is a famous statement, and just like exercise, we know that we feel better when we're making healthier choices. First Corinthians says that our body is a temple, and whether we eat or drink, we should do it for the glory of God. So making good choices with our diet and with our bodies will be of some value to our overall outlook. First Timothy says that bodily training is of some value, but godliness will help you in the present and future life.

Do you need to incorporate physical movement and improve your eating habits? Think about some new choices you can make today?

> Heavenly Father, thank You for giving us instructions for all aspects of life. My body is a temple and should be used for Your glory. I haven't always made the wisest choices with what I eat, what I drink, and how I exercise. Help me today be a better steward of this body! Thank You, Jesus! Amen!

STATE OF GRATITUDE

> Not that I am speaking of being in need, for I have learned in whatever situation I am to be content. I know how to be brought low, and I know how to abound. In any and every circumstance, I have learned the secret of facing plenty and hunger, abundance and need. I can do all things through him who strengthens me.
> —Philippians 4:11–13

Gratitude is the attitude that determines our altitude. I don't know about you, but keeping a grateful heart in any situation is a real challenge. With any email, text, or phone call, I have the capability of going negative with the best of them. Maintaining a grateful outlook is the key to unleashing God's power in our life. In his letter to the Philippians, Paul certainly understood that having an attitude of gratitude was the key ingredient to living a content life. Paul says in Philippians 4 that he has learned that in any situation to be content. Regardless of his financial status, despite being hungry, no matter if he has plenty or if he's in great need, we are to be content. Did you catch that in verse 13? He has "learned" to be content? That suggests being content is a learned behavior. We can decide to be grateful. Being content is something that we make a conscious decision to choose gratefulness. We can maintain attitude of gratefulness regardless of our current situation. One way to maintain an attitude of gratitude is by practicing. When you start feeling your mind drifting to the negative zone, take a gratitude walk. Start listing everything that you have to be thankful for. If you will open your mind to what God is doing around you, you can quickly find that gratitude list will be quite long.

But how are we able to maintain this constant attitude of gratitude? Through Him, through Christ Jesus Who strengthens us. It is only through His strength that we can be thankful, grateful, and content in any situation. This should be comforting. Sales are down, gratitude. Sales are up, gratitude. Big purchase order, gratitude. Loss of a customer, gratitude. Job change, gratitude. Through Christ Jesus that strengthens me!

Have you made a gratitude list? Start today with a list of everything that you are thankful for. Take a gratitude walk today!

> Lord Jesus, thank You for giving me a new outlook on life today. I confess that I don't always have an attitude of gratitude. Help me to look at the positive things in my life and be thankful. I praise Your name for helping me to develop a new attitude! In Jesus's name! Amen!

FOR ME, NOT TO ME

> What then shall we say to these things? If
> God is for us, who can be against us?
> —Romans 8:31

A key principle for maintaining a great outlook in life is determined by how you view opportunities. When you're faced with a challenging situation, do you immediately default to a "why is this happening to me" attitude? Or do you embrace each situation and face it from a "this is being done for me" perspective? Genesis 50:20 says, "As for you, you meant evil against me, but God meant it for good, to bring it about that many people should be kept alive, as they are today." As a follower in Christ, we can have the confidence that God is working for us, and He intends good for us. This does not minimize the pain, suffering, or even loss that you may experience; but it's owning the precept that God is good and claiming that whatever comes my way it is meant for the good for those that are in Christ Jesus.

I have a friend that was let go from his company the week of Christmas. He had performed well, was well respected from his customers, and he typically always hit his quota, but for some reason, the company decided to make a change. He made a decision to stand on God's promises and embrace the change with an outlook that what was meant to harm him God intended for his good. He was in the job search mode for several months, and his trust was definitely pushed to the max. There was a lot of those silent moments when he said, "What are you doing, Lord?" But he remained steadfast, and God was faithful. He helped place him in a role that he would never have looked for on his own. In speaking to my friend today, he loves what he's doing and has great fulfillment from his job. Interesting enough, the person they replaced with him lasted less than a year and never sold one thing. How ironic?

How do you view life's opportunities? Can you own Romans 8:31 today and say, "If God is for me, who can be against me"?

> Thank you, Father, for your constant faithfulness. Even when I display doubt, you are working on my behalf! Help me to own the fact that you are for me and not against me. Change my attitude from looking at challenges that are being done to me and help me to embrace the unknown! Thank You for Your faithfulness, Lord. I love You, Jesus! Amen!

PRAY WITHOUT CEASING

> Rejoice always, pray without ceasing, give thanks in all circumstances; for this is the will of God in Christ Jesus for you.
> —1 Thessalonians 5:16–17

When should we pray? One of the quickest ways to learn when we should pray is to become a 100 percent commissioned sales rep. First Thessalonians says we are to pray without ceasing. If your job performance and family income is based completely on what you sell, then I would venture a guess that you have learned the value of constant prayer. Lose a major account, have a terrible month, fall behind on your annual quota, fail to meet your sales goals, or have one of your best customers start sending their business to your biggest competitor; and you will quickly be praying to God for help. I don't know about you, but some of my closest moments with God have come when I don't know how or where the next sale is going to come from. It's easy to praise the Lord when you're tracking way ahead of plan, but start falling behind, and that's where you'll learn the lesson of constant prayer. James 1:12 says, "Blessed is the man who remains steadfast under trial." How do we pray without ceasing? You may say, "I can't pray all day. I have to work at some point." Well, it's about remaining in a constant mindset of prayer. Pray when you rise, pray when we go to bed, pray in the shower, pray when we brush our teeth, pray when you eat, and pray when you drive. Send prayers of praise when you're in traffic or sitting at a red light. Pray in your car before a meeting; send a prayer of thanks after the meeting. Pray for your coworkers, pray for your neighbors, pray for your family, and pray for your customers. It doesn't have to be some long, drawn-out prayer in Hebrew. Your prayer may be as simple as a quick "Thank You, Lord" or just "Help me, Lord."

If you have a wife, husband, or kids, if you're a brother, sister, or have a mom or dad, you know the power of prayer is not limited to your sales profession alone. I recently learned the lesson that Romans 12:12 teaches, "Rejoice in hope, be patient in tribulation, be constant in payer." I was reminded of this lesson of praying without ceasing with my ten-year-old. He had been having some behavioral issues for several weeks, and I thought they had subsided. As it always goes, I was in my car on the phone in the driveway just telling a friend of mine how it looked like he had made a turn for the good, only to walk in the house and see my son having a complete meltdown. Not just a minor storm but a complete demon-possessed, losing-his-mind, "I don't recognize him" major fit of rage. I immediately was reminded that I had slacked off on praying for him. I thought in my mind, "Well, I've got that one handled. We have that one behind us. Let's move on to the next problem." God wants us to bring everything to him by prayer and petition, with thanksgiving to present our requests to God (Philippians 4:6).

Do you pray without ceasing? Remind yourself today to be in constant prayer.

....

> Lord, I often think that I have everything handled. I come before You to confess that I don't have it all figured out. There are times in my life that I don't have the answers. I need You. I need the Holy Spirit to be guiding me in every aspect of my life. Be with me, Lord! In Jesus's name I pray! Amen.

RANDOM ACTS OF KINDNESS

> But as you excel in everything—in faith, in speech, in knowledge, in all earnestness, and in our love for you—see that you excel in this act of grace also.
> —2 Corinthians 8:7

The Bible is filled with examples of individuals showing random acts of kindness to others. The stories range from the Good Samaritan to Boaz with Ruth to Rebecca providing water to Eliezer for him and his camels. The Bible is filled with examples of people helping others just because it's the right thing to do. Now I don't know of a lot of people riding camels today that you can provide water for them, but the principle of showing random kindness to a stranger still exists.

In Matthew 25, it says that whatever we do for the least of these, we are doing for Christ Himself. If we give them something to drink, provide clothes, look after the sick or visit a prisoner, we are being the hands and feet of Christ. In John 13:34, Jesus gives us a new commandment and that is that we love one another. Although this new commandment did not abolish the original ten, Jesus is saying we must show love to each other, be kind to each other, show compassion for others, and be decent to strangers. Over the years, there have been all kinds of taglines for showing kindness to others. Mottos like "pay it forward," "hugs for thugs," "be a go-giver," "thousand points of light" or "random acts of kindness," to name a few. Jesus Christ showed the ultimate "pay it forward" example in that He laid down his life for us on the cross that if we believe we might have eternal life. What are some ways that we can show love to one another? We can start by showing kindness to each other. Luke 6:35 says, "But love your enemies, and do good, and lend, expecting nothing in return, and your reward will be great, and you will be sons of the Most High, for he is kind to the ungrateful and the evil." Do something kind for a complete stranger and see how it will light up their face. It's a simple principle that when we help others without conditions attached to it, we are the ones that reap the greatest reward. I think you will find that by helping others or showing kindness to a stranger, it not only is the right thing to do, but you will fill your happiness tank all the way to the top. Now that's a win-win for everyone!

Can you think of some ways that you can show kindness to others today? Start with something simple and be a go-giver. Do a random act of kindness today.

> Jesus, thank You for setting the greatest example of unconditional love by dying on the cross for me. Help me to consider others more highly than myself and to serve others each day. Let me be the hands and feet of Christ today! Thank You for loving me! In Jesus's name I pray! Amen!

WHAT WENT WELL TODAY

> Trust in the Lord with all your heart and lean not on your own understanding; in all your ways submit to him and He will make your paths straight.
> —Proverbs 3:5–6

Maintaining and keeping a grateful heart and the right attitude is not easy. Life throws at you a lot of curveballs and potholes. One simple way to maintain the right perspective is, at the end of every day, reflect back on what went well today. I'm not saying every day is going to be cotton candy and puffy white clouds. There are no doubt those days that you feel like the only thing that went well was you woke up. You may even feel like "I wish I had stayed in bed all day." Well, there's one thing to be thankful for: You have a bed. There are those days that are a real stretch to name what went well today. I may have to include the simple things like the tires on the car had air in them today. Trust me, if you've ever been running out the door, late for a meeting, and had a flat tire on your car, you will quickly realize having inflated tires every day is a good thing. But I think, when you start with an attitude of gratefulness, you will quickly see that a lot of things go well each and every day.

On NBC's *Tonight Show*, the former host, Johnny Carson, read an item from the lost-and-found column of a Midwestern newspaper: "Lost dog—brown fur, some missing due to mange, blind in one eye, deaf, lame leg due to recent traffic accident, slightly arthritic. Goes by the name of 'Lucky." At least we hope "Lucky" found his owners. Does that feel like you some days? Instead of having our focus on what operations did wrong, our company doesn't value us, how you're never going to hit quota, the new commission program stinks, distribution doesn't stock product, our company can't get product out on time, customers are price shopping you, your products are out of date, how we lost a big sale, or perhaps we had a flat tire or ran out of gas, was late for our meetings, traffic was terrible or whatever the wide variety of reasons we go negative. If we turn the thoughts around and start reflecting on what went well each and every day, you will quickly see how those negative attitudes can be replaced with an attitude of gratitude.

What went well today? Start making a mental list each and every day of things that turned out good.

....

> Dear heavenly Father, thank You for all good things that I take for granted each and every day. Help me to have a new attitude. Bring back to my mind all the good things that went well each and every day. Thank You for caring about the smallest details of my life! In Jesus's name I pray! Amen!

BREVITY OF LIFE

Come now, you who say, "Today or tomorrow we will go into such and such a town and spend a year there and trade and make a profit"—yet you do not know what tomorrow will bring. What is your life? For you are a mist that appears for a little time and then vanishes. Instead you ought to say, "If the Lord wills, we will live and do this or that." As it is, you boast in your arrogance. All such boasting is evil. So whoever knows the right thing to do and fails to do it, for him it is sin.
—James 4:13–17

Life is short! I have learned this lesson multiple times in my life. Several years ago, I had a series of seizures, and in one episode while I was in intensive care, my heart stopped for 19.6 seconds. When your heart stops for 19.6 seconds, what is more important, the heart or the brain? The neurologist would say the brain since it tells the heart to pump the blood. The cardiologist would say the heart since without blood the brain can't function. I would suggest the theologian is correct. If your heart or brain ceases to function, your soul lives on. That is the most important question to answer. What happens when we die? Praise be to the Lord, my heart restarted on its own, and I have been seizure free ever since.

More recently, while driving to see a customer, my car veered off the interstate in a construction zone, went down an embankment, and headfirst into a tree. Both airbags deployed and the car destroyed, but amazingly enough, I walked away. The only scratch I had was on my leg from a briar when getting out of the car. James 4 says, "We do not know what tomorrow brings." Life can change in a blink of an eye. We are not promised even the next breath.

For those of us that spend a lot of time in our car or airplane flying to our next meeting, we often take for granted our safety. The reality is, every time we jump in the car, there's a chance for an accident. There are over 10 million car accidents every year in the US alone. What I found interesting was just a few miles before my crash, I was on the phone with a coworker who was going through a health struggle. I had just reminded him that we have no promise of our next breath. Those words had just rolled off my tongue when, just a few miles later, bam! Confidence and fear of the Lord must coexist in our lives. The Lord wants us to live in confidence, but we must have a healthy respect and fear of the Lord. In our sales role, we can worry about a lot of things. Most sales professionals I know have a certain level of anxiety, stress, and worry most of the time. I understand the pressure that sales can produce, but let's keep in mind that we have no promise of our next breath. Embrace the moment and love the Lord!

Are you guilty of taking life for granted? Take time today to be thankful and grateful for the next breath you take!

> Lord, I am guilty of taking life's precious moments for granted. I don't always embrace the moment. Thank You, Lord, for Your daily protection. Thank You for watching over my life. Keep me safe today! In Jesus's name I pray! Amen!

LAUGHTER IS GOOD MEDICINE

A joyful heart is good medicine, but a
crushed spirit dries up the bones.
—Proverbs 17:22

What is the funniest thing that has ever happened to you in a sales meeting? I have been asked this question in a job interview just to see if I can laugh at myself and if I have a sense of humor. Being able to laugh at yourself and find the humor in things is good for the heart! In the course of my sales career, I've had more than my share of funny moments. Like the time when I was a boat salesman and during the National Sales meeting, I wrecked a $100,000 boat. Right there in front of everyone, I accidentally put the boat in reverse and at full speed I beached that thing. It completely destroyed the props and pretty much ruined the rest of my day. I didn't think it was so funny, and I don't think the boat company found it humorous, but everyone got a great laugh that week. I can remember another time when I was in a meeting and had to run out to my car to grab something that I had forgotten. We were sitting in an all-glass conference room. As I ran out, yep, you guessed it, headfirst right into the glass door. Everyone thought I was goofing off, but I totally plowed right into that door. I've had more than my fair share of sales meetings where I look down and I'm wearing two completely different socks. If you're thinking, "Jeez, this guy has certainly had his share of embarrassing sales moments." You would be correct. You gotta be able to laugh at the situation.

Proverbs says a joyful heart is good medicine, but a crushed spirit dries up the bones. Don't you feel better when you're laughing? I mean a good, make-you-cry belly laugh? Preschool kids don't have to be told to laugh. On average, a kid laughs three hundred times a day compared to only seventeen times a day for adults. That's an average. I know of some adults that haven't laughed seventeen times in a year or maybe even a lifetime. Think about that. Kids laugh twenty times more every day than we do as adults. Laughter is good for the heart! Laughter decreases stress hormones and increases immune cells and infection-fighting antibodies, thus improving your resistance to disease. Laughter triggers the release of endorphins, the body's natural feel-good chemicals. Endorphins promote an overall sense of well-being and can even temporarily relieve pain. Next time something embarrassing happens in a sales meeting, see if you can find the humor in it. It will put a smile on your face!

What's the funniest thing that ever happened to you? Take some time and think about some funny stories that you remember.

> Lord, thank You for giving us humor. Help me look at life with a sense of laughter. Let me help put a smile on someone else's face today! In Jesus's name! Amen!

KUDZU VINE

> Therefore, since we are surrounded by so great a
> cloud of witnesses, let us also lay aside every weight,
> and sin which clings so closely, and let us run
> with endurance the race that is set before us,
> —Hebrews 12:1

    I live in an area where I have kudzu growing in my backyard. In case you're not familiar with this pesty little vine, it can grow as fast as a foot per day and up to sixty feet every season. Sometimes I truly believe I can see it growing before my eyes. We have a natural area behind our house, and if left untreated, the kudzu just takes over. This past fall, I was trimming back the kudzu. You have to cut it at the root if you want to destroy it. As I began to cut the roots, I noticed one had wrapped itself around one of our magnolia trees. It had entangled itself so tightly around the tree that it was choking the tree. When I was able to finally cut the root off the tree and untangle it from the tree, it had left its mark on the entire trunk of that tree. That trunk will never be the same and will always bear the mark of the kudzu vine. That's the way sin is in our life. If we are not careful to separate ourselves from sin, it can entangle our lives so closely, it will cling to our life so closely that it will grow around the "tree trunk" of our life leaving its mark permanently.

    As we go about our sales jobs, it's easy to let the sin of the world intermingle in our life. We have all heard the numerous stories of sales reps cheating on their spouses only to have their families completely destroyed. Leaving a permanent mark on their family forever. Or how about the infamous national sales meetings where individuals get so out of control, they can barely function the next day. They seem to live by the rule of what "goes out of town, stays out of town" or "what goes to Vegas stays in Vegas." A lot of reps feel compelled to compromise their moral standards or Christian principles just to make a sale. They feel pressured to join in on the vulgar "water cooler" conversations or cave in to pressure to cheat or lie. Hebrews 12 says we are surrounded by a cloud of witnesses, and the race that is set before us is an endurance race. And verse 2 says how do we do this? By looking to Jesus, the founder and perfecter of our faith. Think about the cloud of witnesses we have rooting for us, pulling for us and cheering us on up in heaven. I can imagine Paul, Peter, or my godly grandparents up in heaven, saying, "Come on, Tim, you can do it! We're rooting for you!" Better yet, we have Jesus himself seated at the right hand of the throne of God, encouraging us that we can do it! We are running an endurance race, but the Good News is, we have Jesus Christ himself in our corner sitting at the right hand of God! You can do it!

What are the "kudzu vines" that are ruining your life? Have you been guilty of compromising your beliefs in your sales role? Pray today for God to strengthen you and give you the endurance to not give in to those temptations.

> Jesus, thank You for being our intercessor at the throne of God! Thank You for setting the example that we can run this endurance race called life! Thank You for giving me strength to overcome the pressures of my job and draw a moral line in the sand. Thank You for providing! In Jesus's name! Amen!

AWKWARD MOMENTS

> Then Balaam said to the angel of the Lord, "I have sinned, for I did not know that you stood in the road against me. Now therefore, if it is evil in your sight, I will turn back."
> —Numbers 22:34

The story of Balaam talking to his donkey in Numbers 22 is one of the more bizarre stories in the Bible. I have more than my fair share of bizarre moments throughout my sales career. One moment that I can remember came during a sales meeting with a customer that I was in along with my boss at the time. We met the customer and conducted our meeting in these large chairs located in the lobby. My client was sitting in the chair beside me with my boss sitting across from me. As the meeting went on, I leaned in to show the customer a product in our catalogue. All of a sudden, I felt his hand on my leg, not my knee but my upper thigh. My face probably turned three shades of red from embarrassment. My mind is racing a thousand miles an hour thinking, "What is he doing? What's going on here?" Now I think he accidentally placed his hand on my leg, thinking it was the armchair, but for what felt like hours, his hand was resting on my leg. From that second on, I didn't hear another word he was saying. He sounded like Charlie Brown's teacher to me. All I could think to myself was, "Do not look up at my boss or we both are going to bust out in laughter." When my boss and I finally made it to the parking lot, neither one of us could contain ourselves. It's been years now, and every time I chat with my old boss, we both just start laughing retelling the story. Bizarre!

I think the story with Balaam talking to his donkey certainly tops mine for bizarre. We find Balaam deciding to saddle up his donkey and go face the Moabites after God had told him to do only what He told him to do. Balaam decides to do it his own way. Well, to make his point, God allows the donkey to see these angels standing in the road. So the donkey veers off the road to avoid the angel multiple times and one time pushes Balaam's leg against a wall. So Balaam and the donkey start talking to each other. Now that's different! Growing up in Kentucky, I've seen more than one guy talking to a horse, but I can't say I've heard anyone say they've had one talk back or at least anyone that was sober-minded at the time. I'm sure once God opened Balaam's eyes and he saw the angel of the Lord, he thought to himself, *I was just talking to my donkey and even more bizarre, my donkey was talking back to me. I need a rest!* God was getting Balaam's attention. When God is trying to get our attention, He may choose to use any method He decides. After all, He's God! I have often said, "If God can speak through a donkey, then maybe he can use me as well." Look for God in the bizarre today. Listen for him in the awkward moments. See if he is in the unique. It may be possible that God is using the unusual to get your attention. After all, God used a donkey to get Balaam's attention.

Have you ever had an awkward moment? Look for God in the bizarre today. What is God trying to get your attention about?

....

Lord, thank You for using the bizarre. I don't always recognize what You're doing around me. Help me to be more aware today! Thank you, Jesus! Amen!

THINK BEFORE YOU SPEAK

> Be not rash with your mouth, nor let your heart be hasty
> to utter a word before God, for god is in heaven and
> you are on earth. Therefore let your words be few.
> —Ecclesiastes 5:2

Telling a sales rep to let our words be few is like telling a fisherman to not catch fish. Talking is what we do. But there is a sales principle in choosing our words wisely before we speak. There's a well-documented with an eyewitness to the story about a manufacturer's representative in my industry who was once on a sales call. The meeting was going well, and the customer and rep exchanging conversation talking about music, guitars, and rock bands. About that time, the sales rep notices a picture sitting behind the client's desk. He asks him, "Is that Tom Petty with you in the picture?" The customer quickly responds, "No, that's my wife." The sales rep just said this man's wife looks like Tom Petty. Now Tom Petty was a tremendous musician, but I don't think he would be winning any beauty pageants. Oops, meeting over. Probably an honest mistake given the prior conversation but oh my, what a mistaken use of words.

Selecting our words wisely is a good reminder for any sales rep or for that matter, anyone. This is not isolated to sales meetings only. It's a good idea to not be hasty with our words. Think before we speak. In a sales context, this may apply to avoiding controversial topics unless you absolutely know the position or stance your customer has taken. It may be something as simple as bashing a sports team, only to find out that customer is extremely passionate about his alma mater. I've had to avoid talking about sports with certain customers since they root for the archrival of my favorite team. Banter can all be in good fun, but for the wrong person, it can be a landmine. We've all heard it said to avoid discussion about politics, family, or religion in various contexts. We live in a current time with social media where people feel empowered to say anything they want at any time and hide behind the post regardless of how it may make someone feel. Ecclesiastes says to be not rash with our mouth. Anything we say, we are saying before God. We should choose our words wisely. Words are like toothpaste; once they are out of the tube, you can't put it back into the container. So let's think before we speak!

Have you been guilty of being quick to speak and slow to listen? Think today before we speak.

....

> Lord, You are an all-knowing God. Thank You for caring about our words. Let me choose my words wisely today. Let everything I say be glorifying to Your name! In Jesus's precious name I pray! Amen!

IN THE WHISPER

And he said, "Go out and stand on the mount before the Lord." And behold, the Lord passed by, and a great and strong wind tore the mountains and broke in pieces the rocks before the Lord, but the Lord was not in the wind. And after the wind an earthquake, but the Lord was not in the earthquake. And after the earthquake a fire, but the Lord was not in the fire. And after the fire the sound of a low whisper.
—1 Kings 19:11–12

Hearing God's voice clearly speak to us can be one of the most frustrating things we experience in our Christian walk. Waiting on the Lord and listening for His voice will develop more faith muscles than feeding thousands of homeless people. We want to hear God in a loud, audible voice. For most people and most of the time, God only whispers. I like to watch University of Kentucky basketball. But sometimes, when I'm traveling in my car and the game is on, I will turn my radio on to see if I can listen to the game. Now keep in mind, I live in North Carolina, and finding a radio station that will broadcast the game is next to impossible. There's one AM station based in Kentucky that broadcasts UK basketball games. For most AM radio stations, you can only pick up the signal a few miles from the actual broadcast. This station, however, pumps out 50,000 watts. I live hundreds of miles away from the radio station and, most times, can't pick up this station. But on a clear, cool, quite evening, sometimes I can pick the broadcast up as clear as being next to the station. That's the way it is when God speaks. He may be pumping out 50,000 watts, but we're so far away that it requires us to get alone and be real quite in order to hear from Him. I have experienced times in my life when God has spoken in a whisper months before something actually happens. If I'm being honest, most times I dismiss this whisper only to see months later the exact thing God was saying come about. I have to learn to not only listen for God's voice, but I must be able to hear God's whisper. When He speaks, I must learn to accept in faith, obey, and wait on the Lord.

It would great for God to speak to us so loud that it shakes us like an earthquake or blow so much it feels like a strong wind is going to blow us over or light up our life like a bright, glowing fire but as 1 Kings says, "He comes in a whisper." What is God whispering to you today? Maybe you need to get alone, remove the noise, and listen for the whisper. Have you heard God whisper and now you need to obey? Get alone with God, spend time with God, and listen for the whisper.

Can you hear God whisper? What can you do today to get quite and listen for his voice?

....

> Lord, thank You for whispering to us! Help me to remove the noise, distractions, and clutter in my mind to be able to hear from You. I confess that I don't always spend time with You alone. Help me this day to clearly hear from You. In Jesus's name!

HAVE A PLAN

And the Lord answered me: "Write the vision; make it plain on tablets, so he may run who reads it. For still the vision awaits its appointed time; it hastens to the end—it will not lie. If it seems slow, wait for it: it will surely come; it will not delay.
—Habakkuk 2:2–3

How do you measure a successful day as a sales rep? Most sales reps are measured by purchase orders or by sales invoices. This is a valid discussion point since as a sales professional, it is our job to sale. After all, no company can continue to be in business without sales. I suggest, however, that sales is simply a by-product of quality activities. We have all heard quotes about plans such as "A goal without a plan is just a wish" or "By failing to prepare, you are preparing to fail." You have to have a plan every day, every month, and every year for your sales success. Planning and having a daily sales plan is biblical. Habakkuk 2:2 says to write the vision down and make it plain.

I would suggest having a point system to measure your activities every day. I utilize a system that I call Work Watchers, "Have a Good Day" System. The system consists of assigning a point value to the various sales tasks that I must perform each day. For example, cold calls = 1 point, follow-up call = 2 points, networking relationship calls = 5 points, setting an appointment = 10 points, appointment kept = 15 points, and a customer visit = 5 points. "A good day" consists of at least 50 points. Notice there are no point values assigned for administrative tasks, and there are no points assigned for receiving a purchase order. As I stated, sales is simply the by-product of quality activities. This is a suggested plan and can be modified for your specific sales role. Jeremiah 29:11 says, "'For I know the plans I have for you,' declares the Lord, 'plans to prosper you and not to harm you, plans to give you hope and a future.'" God has a plan for you and for your life. As a professional sales rep, we should have a plan for our daily sales activities.

Do you have a daily plan? How can you customize your company's vision into a daily sales activity plan?

....

> Lord, thank You for having a plan for me, for my family, and for my life. I can have confidence that Your plans are perfect. Give me the vision for my life and help me to develop a strategy for succeeding in my job. Thank You for Your provisions! In Jesus's name I pray! Amen!

GOD, I CAN'T HEAR YOU

> Let me hear what God the Lord will speak, for
> he will speak peace to his people, to his saints;
> but let them not turn back to folly.
>
> —Psalm 85:8

Lord, I can't hear you seems to be a battle cry that I scream on a regular basis. It comes like a flood of emotions and a repeating cycle in my life. I have a challenge or request that I think has a deadline. I pray about it, wait patiently for what I think is an appropriate time, only to have no answer, then my frustrations begin, and the next thing I know, I have myself worked up into a frenzy. Is this a familiar cycle for you as well? It's during these times that I just feel like I can't hear from God. It's in these times that my groans, cries, and screams just don't seem to reach God's throne. I am not alone. In Job chapter 3, after sitting for seven days in silence, he finally opens his mouth and in verse 11 says, "Why didn't I just die at birth? Why didn't I expire in my mother's womb?" Can you relate to these thoughts? I know when we are putting on our holy hat and acting all Christian-like, we want to quote those verses about "It's all in God's will," "Be patient and wait on the Lord," or say things like it will all work out; but deep down inside, we're hurting and wondering, "God, why can't I hear You?"

For me, a lot of these thoughts and emotions are centered around my work life. You get off to a slow start in your year and you're wondering, where are You, God? You battle the "sales prevention internal department" every day and you wonder, where are You, God? One of your good customers decides to shop you out to a competitor after years of supporting them and you wonder, God, where are You? For me and a ton of sales reps that are Christians, their work life is what creates the most challenges, frustrations, and even doubts about their walk with the Lord and their faith in God. For me, it can be a vicious cycle that repeats over and over when you least expect it, only to have the feeling of regret, defeat, or discouragement settle in after the wave of emotions is gone.

When you just feel like you can't hear God, let me suggest six things you can do:

1. Genuinely seek His voice.
2. Get as quiet and still as possible.
3. Learn how to listen for His voice.
4. Maintain a humble heart.
5. Believe and trust that God wants to speak to you.
6. Don't ever forget that God loves you.

I know it's easier said than done, but if as soon as that clanging, annoying noise of discouragement starts showing up in your head, double down on these two things: 1 John 4:18 says, "There is no fear in love, but perfect love cast out fear. For fear has to do with punishment, and whoever fears has been perfected in love." And always remember Proverbs 3:5: "Trust in the Lord with all your heart, and do not lean on your own understanding." We just can't trust our own feelings and emotions when life comes flooding in.

What are your typical reactions when you don't feel like you're hearing from God?

> Lord, I confess that when I get discouraged and my feelings take over like an ocean wave, I don't always trust You. I am sorry, Lord! Help me, Lord, to increase my trust in You even when I don't think I'm hearing from You. Thank You for being a god of love and a god Who loves me! I love You, Lord! Amen!

SEEK HIS VOICE

Call to me and I will answer you, and will tell you great and hidden things that you have not known.
—Jeremiah 33:3

The Bible is filled with examples of God speaking various individuals such as Noah, Abram, Moses, Isaiah, Samuel, Ezekiel, David, Jacob, Solomon, Elijah, Jonah, Hosea, Zechariah, John, Paul, Peter, and the list goes on. From the very beginning, after God created Adam, they had a relationship and God would speak to Adam. In Genesis 3, Adam and Eve heard the sound of the Lord walking in the Garden in the cool of the day, and God called out to them asking, "Where are you?" In order to hear God's voice, we must be listening for His voice. We must genuinely and humbly seek His voice. Psalm 91:15 says, "When you call to me, I will answer you. I will be with you when you are in trouble. I will save you and honor you." God's voice may come in the form of a whisper, thunder, a storm, or a gentle wind. It may sound similar to a voice that you're familiar with. It may come from the counsel of a friend, family member, or even in the very nature He created. Psalm 29:3–9 says, "The Lord's voice is on the waters, in thunder, it is powerful, it breaks the cedars, it divides the flames, shakes the wilderness, and discovers the forests." God may speak in a variety of ways, and God still speaks to us today. Although God may choose to speak to you in any way He chooses, He gave us his word to speak directly to you and me. John 10:27 declares, "My Sheep hear my voice, and I know them, and they follow me." If we want to clearly hear from God, we must know Him and genuinely and humbly seek Him. Jeremiah says if we call to Him, He will answer you. Call to Him today!

Do you need to hear God's voice today? Start by humbly seeking Him first!

....

> God our Father, You are all-powerful and all-knowing. You know my inner thoughts, desires, and needs. I humbly bow before You and ask to hear from You. I need to hear from You, Lord. I ask that You guide me, direct me, and lead me. Put people in my path that intend good, and remove the people that intend harm. Let me walk in Your perfect will. In the precious name of Jesus I pray! Amen!

BE STILL AND KNOW

> He says, "Be still and know that I am God: I will be
> exalted among nations, I will be exalted in the earth."
> —Psalm 46:10

Jesus gave us many examples of Him breaking away from the crowd, being by Himself, getting real quiet, and spending time alone. Jesus understood the value of solitude. Jesus understood that every so often, you just have to get away, block out the noise, and enjoy the silence in order to spend time alone with God our Father. Jesus would often be found walking by the water (Mark 1:16), alone in a solitary place (Mark 1:35), praying by Himself (Luke 5:15–16), by the lake (Mark 2:13, Mark 6:31–32), on a mountain (Luke 6:12–13, Mark 9:2), in a garden (Mark 14:32), and many other examples. Jesus shows us the power of just getting away from the clutter, the white noise, our chatterbox going off in our heads, and the crowds to quality time alone with God the Father.

My wife often accuses me of zoning out during our conversations. She can see that dazed look in my eyes. I'm always quick with the response that I'm just meditating, but the reality is, my mind is on that deserted island, laying on a beach, enjoying the sun, and taking in the peace and quiet. Psalm 46:10 says to "be still and know that I am God." It is important to have quiet time, really get alone, enjoy the solitude, and listen for God's voice. It is majorly important when you are desperately trying to hear God's voice to break away from the noise and to get real quiet. Being still allows us to charge up our battery, push the reset button, and refresh our soul. It allows God to speak to us in a voice that can only be heard in the stillness and quietness of solitude. You're probably saying, "How in the world am I going to get away to a mountain or a lake? I have kids running everywhere; emails, texts, phone calls, TV blaring in the background;

Fortnite playing; pots and pans banging in the kitchen. I can't even hear myself think!" My answer…that's exactly my point! Matthew 6:5–6 we should go into our room or a prayer closet and spend time alone with our Father. If you are in a sales role that requires you to drive, turn the phone off, radio off, and just enjoy the silence. Perhaps there's a room in your house that you can designate your own personal prayer closet, put your headphones without music, and take a walk, plan to arrive at a meeting early and sit quietly in your car. Point being, when you really need to hear God's voice, we must get quiet. Be intentional, recognize the need to be quiet, and set aside that time.

Do you have special time set aside to be still and hear from God? Be intentional today to have some alone time with God!

....

> God, thank You for giving us direct access to you. We can come to You with all our cares, needs, hurts, and problems; and You care. Help me to embrace the quietness, the solitude, and to hear from You. Thank You for hearing me, Lord. In Jesus's name I pray. Amen!

RECOGNIZE HIS VOICE

My sheep hear my voice, and I know
them, and they follow me.
—John 10:27

In the book of 1 Samuel 3, the Bible tells a story of Samuel confusing God's voice with that of Eli's. God spoke to Samuel three times, and he kept mistaking God's voice for that of Eli. After the third time, Eli realized that it was God speaking to Samuel and told him, "The next time you hear the voice, say 'Speak LORD, for your servant is listening.'" Sometimes God's voice may sound very familiar and similar to other voices that you hear every day. In Samuel's case, it sounded like Eli's voice. Samuel couldn't distinguish God's voice to Eli's. It is important to be able to recognize God's voice, first we must learn to hear God's voice and then distinguish that it is God speaking to us. Sometimes it can be hard to discern that its God's voice and not the voice of something else familiar to us. Jeremiah 29:13 says, "You will seek me and find me when you seek me with all your heart." In order to hear God's voice, we must be seeking God's voice and with all our heart. We must also remember that God's primary desire in speaking to us is for His eternal purpose. Sometimes we can get God's voice confused with our own selfish desires, and we rationalize that it must be God speaking to me when it's actually not.

Sometimes it may be easier to understand, discern, and be able to recognize that it is *not* God's voice that we are hearing at all. God is holy and will not violate His own biblical principles. When something doesn't line up with God's word, chances are, it is not God's voice that you are hearing. We all can be guilty of making a decision on our own, then asking God to bless that decision when it clearly violates a core principle in God's word. We rationalize after wrestling with the decision that we must have heard from God only to end up frustrated, confused, and perhaps even in a bad situation. Not only must we recognize God's voice; we must *obey* His voice. I have heard it said that delayed obedience is disobedience. When we hear God's voice, we must be just like Samuel and say, "Yes, Lord, here I am!"

Do you need to hear God's voice today? Start by saying, "Yes, Lord, here I am!"

....

> Lord, help me to recognize Your voice. I need to hear from You today. I ask You to speak to me in a voice that can only be Yours. Teach me to recognize Your voice and to obey You in all that I do. Thank You for loving me! In Jesus's name I pray! Amen!

MAINTAIN A HUMBLE HEART

> Who is wise and understanding among you? Let
> them show it by their good life, by deeds done
> in the humility that comes from wisdom.
> —James 3:13

Charles Spurgeon is quoted as saying, "Think not that humility is weakness; it shall supply the marrow of strength to thy bones. Stoop and conquer; bow thyself and become invincible." In other words, with humility comes great strength. We often think of humility of a sign of weakness that pride, and arrogance is a show of mighty force and strength. We don't have to look very far for examples of individuals that appeared to be extremely confident, proud, and arrogant, only to see them fall and be humiliated. You can open any section of any news report and see examples daily of actors, sports figures, politicians, or world leaders. Pride is not reserved strictly for the rich and famous. Every day in our own life, the root of pride can work its way through the cracks in our own lives. It can seep in through subtle ways; it can be in the form of being proud of a huge sale we just closed, and we want to let everyone that can hear know we just took down a big deal. It can be with a disagreement with a coworker, friend, or spouse, and pride comes rushing in with our overwhelming need to be right. It can even come through some type of ministry opportunity. We want to say, "Look at me over here feeding the homeless. See what a great person I am?"

Philippians 2:3 says, "Do nothing out of selfish ambition or vain conceit. Rather, in humility value others above yourselves." Never confuse being humiliated with humility. Being humiliated comes as a result of having a lack of humility. Having humility is having great strength and is a direct reflection of our trust and fear of the Lord. Proverbs 22:4 says, "Humility is the fear of the Lord; it wages are riches and honor and life." Jesus told his very own disciples in Mark 9:35 that anyone who wants to be first must be the very last, and the servant of all. If we want to hear clearly from the Lord, we must check our pride meter. Chances are, we won't be able to recognize where pride and arrogance has crept into our lives. It becomes majorly important to have a close confidant that will shoot it to you straight. Someone in your life that's not afraid to tell you like it is. Check your pride meter and humbly submit yourself to the Lord.

Do you have a close friend that will shoot it to you straight? Ask God to show you where pride has crept into your life. Humbly ask Him to forgive you!

> Lord, I come before You and ask for Your forgiveness where pride is in my life. Without You, I am nothing. Every good and perfect gift comes from You, Lord. I acknowledge You in my life and say, "Thank You for all the blessing You have given me!" Thank You, Lord, for loving me! In Jesus's name I pray. Amen!

BELIEVE AND TRUST THAT GOD WANTS TO SPEAK TO YOU

Have I not commanded you? Be strong and courageous.
Do not be frightened, and do not be dismayed, for
the LORD your God is with you wherever you go.
—Joshua 1:9

Since the very creation of Adam, God has desired a relationship with the very mankind that He created. God wants to speak with you. God wants to have a relationship with you. In order to hear from God, you must believe that God desires to speak with you and have a relationship with you. You must trust and believe that God wants to speak with you. In the beginning, God spoke with Adam in the garden, He spoke to Moses through a burning bush, Paul heard Him speak on the road to Damascus, He spoke to Samuel, Daniel, and Abraham. There is example after example of God desiring to speak to the very humans He created throughout the Bible. Joshua says that God is with us wherever we go. If God is with us everywhere then God has the ability to speak any time He desires.

So how does God choose to speak? First off, God can choose to speak any way He wants to. After all, He is God! Let me suggest eight ways that God speaks today. First, through his word. Second Timothy 3:16 says that all scripture is God-breathed. Second, through His Son Jesus Christ. Jesus says in John 10:27 that His sheep hear His voice and follow Him. Jesus is the fulfillment of scripture. Third, through creation. Luke 19:40 says that even the stones cry out. I'm sure you have seen a beautiful sunset or scenic mountain or a terrific rainbow and know that God is there. You can feel His presence in nature itself. Fourth, through other believers. God may use your pastor, a friend, a parent, a teacher, or a neighbor to convey a truth. God even spoke through a donkey (Numbers 22:28). Fifth, through music. David sang songs and wrote music. Jehoshaphat appointed people to sing to the Lord (2 Chronicles 20:21). The Bible references trumpets playing, and Ecclesiastes 3:4 says there is a time to sing. Psalms is filled with references singing. God can speak through music. Sixth, through circumstances. Just because you find yourself in a difficult circumstance doesn't necessarily mean that God is speaking directly to you, but rather, God may use the circumstance to get our attention. I don't know about you, but I definitely spend more time in prayer when I am in a situation. Seventh, through the Holy Spirit. John 14:17 says the spirit of truth lives in us, dwells in us, and will be with us. The Holy Spirit serves as a guide for us and giving us direction. And finally eighth, through prayer. God gave us prayer as a gift. As a way to have direct communication with Him, Jesus gave us the model prayer and provided examples of how and when to pray. Even when we don't know what to prayer for, Romans 8:26–28 says the spirit is making intercession for us. The Spirit is praying on our behalf even when we don't know what to pray for.

Remember this: We must trust and believe that God wants to have a relationship with us. God wants to speak to us.

Do you need to hear from God today? Trust and believe that He wants to speak to you!

....

> Lord, I desire to hear from You! I trust Your word that You will never leave me nor forsake me. Speak to me today! Show me You will! In Jesus's name I pray! Amen!

GOD LOVES YOU

> The LORD your God is in your midst, a mighty one who will save; he will rejoice over you with gladness; he will quiet you by his love; he will exult over you with loud signing.
> —Zephaniah 3:17

God loves you. Make no mistake that God is a holy and righteous judge, but God is good. God loves you. He rejoices over you with gladness. God's love is steadfast, unchanging, everlasting, and boundless. It comforts us; it's unfailing, overflowing. It's abounding, fearless, and endures forever. God's love is compassionate, faithful, gracious, patient, kind; and it doesn't boast. It protects, trusts, hopes, and perseveres. God loves you. This key principle that God loves us is one that all of us need to hear and believe! First John 4:19 says, "We love because He first loved us." And Romans 5:8 says that God demonstrates his love for us in this: While we were still sinners, Christ died for us. You see, in order to hear from God, we must believe that God loves us with all of our heart. This opens up the door from heaven to be able to hear from Him.

I think so many of us are guilty of finding ourselves in a situation, and we don't hear directly from God, and we start spiraling down and work ourselves in a place that we just don't believe God loves us. "Jesus loves me; this I know, for the Bible tells me so." This children's song rings in anyone's ears that grew up going to church. You sang this song from the time you could talk. As a child, the concept that God loves us is one we almost assume automatically, but somehow as adults, we can't just innocently assume this is true anymore. We need proof. I know for me, anytime I find myself in a difficult situation, the same two questions always reappear. God is saying, "Do you love Me?" and "Do you trust Me?" Every time I find myself in a confusing situation, and I start getting frustrated that God is not answering my prayer, those same two questions come back to haunt me. First Corinthians 13:13 is probably the most used wedding verse of all time. I would venture to say that it is used in more wedding ceremonies than all other verses combined. "And now these three remain: faith, hope and love. But the greatest of these is love." Love is the greatest. We need to recapture the innocence of that children's song and believe that Jesus loves us. If we will trust this, believe this and actually own this; it will open the key for God to speak to us, and we can hear Him and trust Him.

Do you need to hear from God today? Can you honestly say "God, I love you and I trust you"? Do you believe that God loves you?

....

> Dear gracious heavenly Father, I trust You, and I love You. I believe that You have my best interest in mind. I ask that You be with me today. In Jesus's name I pray! Amen!

KEEP PURSUING

> Then Jesus answered her, "O woman, great is
> your faith! Be it done for you as you desire."
> And her daughter was healed instantly.
> —Matthew 15:28

I recently asked a friend of mine who has been a successful sales representative in the education space for a long time to tell me the two most important sales philosophies that he has learned. He quickly responded with (1) people make a purchase decision when an emotional need has been met, and (2) keep pursuing the opportunity until an absolute "no" has been stated and then still continue. Contained within a story found in Matthew 15:21–28, we find multiple sales principles, including Jesus showing us an example of both an emotional need being met and a lady not taking no for an answer. We find these examples in the story of the Canaanite women that has a daughter that is extremely sick. Jesus has obviously built a reputation in this area that he can heal her. The word has gotten out that Jesus has healing abilities. He has made a name for himself and built up His personal brand if you will. The woman approaches Jesus multiple times to heal her daughter, and every time, Jesus sends her away. It wasn't until the third time the lady approaches Jesus that He actually addresses the illness, and her daughter was healed instantly.

So what are the sales principles that we see in this story? First, Jesus had built a reputation in the area that He has the ability to heal. This is an important sales principle. We must build up our own personal sales brand within your given market. Yes, perhaps we are representing a company, but it is our own personal brand and reputation in your territory that people ultimately are buying from. We should strive to build a reputation for honesty, integrity, and what we represent will actually do what we say it will do. Second, we must create an emotional response to our potential clients before a buying decision will be made. The Canaanite woman created an emotional message that ended up resonating with Jesus. Her daughter was dying, and she repeatedly made an emotional appeal to Jesus. All sales decisions are made when the products or services we represent actually meet an important emotional need for the client. That need and demand is uncovered in our discovery and qualifying phase. Uncovering emotional needs can take a long time. We may get hours, days, and weeks into the sales cycle only to find out what we thought was the perceived need is completely different than the customer's emotional need. A purchase decision will be made when we are able to finally discover what that main emotional need is, and our product or service is actually able to meet that demand. Third, keep pursuing the sales opportunity until the door is absolutely closed, and even then, keep pursuing. The Canaanite woman would not take "no" for an answer. Depending upon your industry, a typical sales cycle may take days, weeks, months, and even years before it is closed. We may go through numerous presentations, offers, objections, and negotiations before a final decision is ever made. Bottom line, keep pursuing!

In the discovery phase, are you finding out what your prospects emotional need may be? Have you given up on a prospective client that you need to reconnect with and keep pursuing?

....

> Lord, thank You for giving us examples of sales principles in Your word. Open the doors that You want me to pursue. Put people in my life that intend good for me and remove the people from my path that intend harm. Help give me the energy and drive to keep pursuing opportunities. Thank You for providing for me and my family. I give You all the praise and honor! In Jesus's name I pray! Amen!

BE QUICK TO APOLOGIZE

> Make every effort to live in peace with everyone and to be holy; without holiness no one will see the Lord.
> —Hebrews 12:14

Benjamin Franklin once said, "Never ruin an apology with an excuse." I recently made a terrible rookie sales mistake. A customer that I have worked with for several years informed me that he would be asking for a price from one of my competitors. I started getting defensive when the distributor that provides our pricing started giving me conflicting information. My normal sales paranoia set in, and after hanging up the phone with my customer and feeling like some things was not as transparent as I would like, quite frankly, I felt like either the customer or my distributor was playing a game with me. In following up with what I thought was my distributor on a phone call, I proceeded to complain about the whole situation and accuse the customer of playing games with me. Well, did you guess what I did? Yes, I had dialed the wrong number. I had accidentally redialed my customer and proceeded to moan, groan, and complain about him to him. I felt more than embarrassed. To make matters worse, when I called back to apologize for my unprofessionalism, he would not take my call. I sent texts, emails, left voice mails, and basically stalked him for days at to no avail. After several days of not returning my messages, I finally decided to take my chances and do a drop in at his office. When I showed up, I simply said I offer no excuses for my behavior. I simply apologized and asked for his forgiveness. I told him, "I am here to face the firing squad and take whatever verbal abuse you want to send my way." To my surprise, he forgave me without any conflict. He said my penance was the days of worrying about the conversation. Now, I could have offered a bunch of excuses as to why I reacted the way I did, but that would have gone nowhere. I simply needed to step up, own my mistake, and face the music. Proverbs 14:9 says, "Fools make fun of guilt, but the godly acknowledge it and seek reconciliation." Owning up my insane mistake, facing my customer head on and offering a sincere apology without any excuses has proven to go further than all the support I've provided them over the years. So maybe you haven't made as big of a bone-headed mistake as I made, but you have something you owe someone an apology for. When we offer our apologies, it's similar to repentance; it removes that burden of wrong we have done and that we're carrying around with us. I encourage you to seek reconciliation, offer your sincere apology without excuses, and face the music!

Are there any mistakes you've made with a customer that you need to seek forgiveness?

> Lord, thank You for showing us the ultimate act of forgiveness through the cross. Search me and see if there is any offensive way in me. Help provide the courage that I need to face the person that I need to apologize to. I love You, Lord! Amen!

FRESH WIND, FRESH FIRE

*If you offer a grain offering of firstfruits to the Lord,
you shall offer for the grain offering of your firstfruits
fresh ears, roasted with fire, crushed new grain.*
—Leviticus 2:14

In the Old Testament in the book of Leviticus, there are specific rules on how the sacrificial offerings were to be presented to the Lord. There is a whole listing of offerings such as a burnt offering, peace offerings, sin offering, guilt offering, and in chapter 2, it details a grain offering. It spells out down to the last detail on what the offering should be; how it should be prepared; how it is to be broken apart; how to pour oil on it, the flour, the salt, and if baked, how to prepare it. No detail is left untold. I'm exhausted just reading about it. Aren't you glad that Christ paid the penalty for our sins, and we are under the New Testament? Regardless that we no longer have a grain offering, the message is still very clear: God wants and requires our firstfruits. He wants our very best. This means our very best effort in our job, with our family, in our worship, and in our life.

I know in our sales role, the daily grind and routines can get burdensome and monotonous. We can get in a real rut if we're not careful and start sliding down that miserable hill and our efforts can become completely lackluster. We crave new motivation and fulfillment. In a song by Mack Brock the lyrics say, "Fresh wind, fresh fire. My one desire is to lift you higher, higher. Oh, how I need you, fresh wind, fresh fire. You are my light and my salvation. You are the one that's made me new." Isn't this what our deep desires are? We want to be made new. We want a fresh fire that burns deep inside our souls. True fulfillment can only come from the Lord. Fulfillment in our jobs, in our families, in our homes, in our neighborhood, and in our life can only come from God. Are you craving a fresh wind and fresh fire in your job? Start by making sure you are bringing your firstfruits to the Lord. Your very best effort. Let God work in your heart and bring you the fulfillment that only He can bring.

Are you craving a fresh fire from the Lord? Ask God today to renew your heart and bring a new sense of joy to your work, home, family, and your life!

> Lord, You are the Creator and King. I ask for fresh wind and fresh fire in my life. I ask for fulfillment that only comes from You. I confess that I don't always bring my best effort, my firstfruits. Help me to have a new, fresh desire for You, Lord! In Jesus's name I pray! Amen!

GET OUT OF THE BOAT!

> He said, "Come." So Peter got out of the boat
> and walked on the water and came to Jesus.
> —Matthew 14:29

Most of us know the story found in Matthew of Peter getting out of the boat when he sees Jesus approaching, only to take his eyes off Jesus, and he began to sink. When Peter began to sink, Jesus reached down, and Peter takes his hand, and they climb back into the boat. Most of the time, the focus is always on Peter and the fact that he took his eyes off Jesus, and this is a valid point in the story. We must always keep our eyes on Jesus. But not to be forgotten is the fact that Peter initially had courage and actually got out of the boat. Would you have gotten out of the boat? What keeps us from getting out of the boat? Is it the same fear that Peter had that caused him to take his eyes off Jesus? Maybe it's the comfort of being in the boat to begin with or perhaps it's the rough water, and we don't want to get wet? Maybe the winds are blowing so hard and the distractions so loud, we can't even hear Jesus saying for us to "come, get out of the boat"? As it relates to your sales profession, what area is Jesus saying, "Get out of the boat"? Is it a new role, a new company, or a new venture? Perhaps it's an old customer that's said no a hundred times, and we need to call on them one more time? Maybe it's getting more training, certifications, or going back to school? Maybe we've been doing our job the same way for so long that we need to "get out of the boat" and form new habits?

So would you have gotten out of the boat? We have all heard the stories of people selling everything they own, moving to a foreign country, never looking back, and being happier than they've ever been. As a matter of fact, a family at our church spoke this past weekend and did exactly that. They have four teenage kids, both he and his wife had great jobs, four cars, a nice home, and yet they sold everything and moved to an isolated area that is so dangerous they couldn't even disclose the village or country they are living in, but they are living more fulfilled lives than ever before. Why? How can this be? Obedience! They got out of the boat. And here I am immediately after the service, overthinking, where are we eating today? I go on with my daily activities staying in the boat. Now I don't think that all people are called to move to a remote, isolated foreign country, but we are all called to do something. There is something that God is asking us to trust Him about and to get out of the boat. What is it for you? Let's get out of that boat, keep our eyes on Jesus, and walk on water together!

What is God laying on your heart that He wants you to do? Anything in your work life? What about your personal and spiritual life? Let's have the courage to get out of that boat!

....

> Lord, give me the courage to get out of the boat. Lay on my heart the ideas, plans, and thoughts that are clearly from You. Help me to keep my eyes on You even if the waves are rough and the winds are blowing. Help me to trust You! In Jesus's name I pray! Amen!

EMBRACE MONDAYS

> Satisfy us in the morning with your steadfast love, that we may rejoice and be glad all our days. Let the favor of the Lord our God be upon us, and establish the work of our hands upon us; yes, establish the work of our hands!
> —Psalm 90:14, 17

Do you dread Monday mornings? I know for a lot of salespeople, the mere thought of Monday morning can affect their entire Sunday. Sunday is ruined with the slightest thought of having to get after it Monday morning. Just the thought of starting a new week all over with cold calls, setting appointments, follow-up sales calls, the Monday team kickoff conference call, updating your weekly pipeline, entering meeting records, or challenging yourself to prospecting new accounts or you name it; and dread starts setting in. I'm exhausted already! It's easy to slip into that mindset of dread instead of having that attitude of gratitude and embracing the week. I get it, it's easy to become discouraged instead of having those thankful feelings. It's easy to take for granted that we can even get up out of bed in the morning, that we have a bed to sleep in and that we have a job that we can go to. I know for me, as the week picks up speed and starts building momentum, it becomes easier to find that motivation.

Psalm 90 asks God to satisfy us in the morning with his steadfast love. Let's start to make a shift in our thinking and let Monday mornings be a reminder of God's steadfast love. Verse 17 says to "let the favor of the Lord our God be upon us and establish the work of our hands upon us; yes, establish the work of our hands!" One way to embrace Monday's is start off first thing with praising the Lord and asking Him to establish the work of our hands for the week. Put God first and allow Him to establish your plans. I was told one time that when you have dread of picking up the phone to call new customers, pick out some of your very best customers, the one's that really like working with you and call them. Start off your Monday by letting your very best customers know how much you appreciate them. Give them a call or send them a quick email, letting them know that value them. It may help brighten their day, and it will provide you with some affirmation and perhaps give you the confidence to reach out to new ones. Another quick suggestion is, instead of focusing on the mountain ahead of you, is to start off with some small, easily measured objectives that you can accomplish first thing. As a sales rep, Mondays can feel like an isolated time. Let's make that mindset shift and embrace Mondays and let God satisfy us with his steadfast love!

Are you guilty of dreading Monday mornings? What shifts in your mindset can you make to embrace Mondays?

....

> Lord, thank You for Mondays. I confess that I take for granted the very fact that I am able to get up this morning! Thank You for providing for all my needs. I ask that You help me be focused on your faithfulness and steadfast love. I ask that You establish the work of my hands. Bless my customers and bless my coworkers today. Put people in my path that intend good for me and change the hearts of the one's that intend harm. Let me be a light for Your today. In Jesus's name I pray! Amen!

FAILURE DOESN'T DISQUALIFY YOU

> And the Lord turned and looked at Peter. And Peter remembered the saying of the Lord, how he had said to him, "Before the rooster crows today, you will deny me three times." And he went out and wept bitterly.
> —Luke 22:61–62

Everyone has faced those times in their sales careers when they felt like a failure. Maybe you were let go from a position for not meeting expectations. Perhaps you failed to close that big deal your boss was expecting or maybe you lost a major account. Regardless of the circumstances, the situation left you feeling like you had failed, or perhaps you actually did fail to meet the goal. Sometimes our biggest failures come immediately following a major victory. One minute you're high-fiving each other, and the next you feel like someone stole your dog. These thoughts of failure can leave us feeling powerless.

Luke records a story of Peter's epic failure when he denied knowing Christ. When the guards came to arrest Jesus, to defend Jesus, Peter drew his sword and cut off one of the soldiers' ears. At that moment, he was bold and fearless. Ironically, not long after this encounter, Peter was in the courtyard where Jesus was being questioned. Peter not only denies he knows Jesus once; he does it three times. One of the denials, the Bible says, was to a little girl. Imagine that: Peter cut off a soldier's ear and could have been killed for so doing and then, out of fear, denies even knowing Jesus to a kid. This must have created a feeling of complete failure within Peter.

Now, it would be one thing if the story had ended there, but Peter's failure did not disqualify him from future service. Jesus ends up reaffirming Peter in front of all the disciples after His resurrection (as recorded in John 21). And in Acts 4, we see Peter's renewed boldness as he stood before the council with boldness. The Bible even says his prayers shook the building. Now that's a tremendous turnaround! What does this mean for you? *Your past failures do not have to define your future success.*

If you find yourself having been part of an epic failure, this does not have to be the final chapter in your sales career or in your life. Own the mistake, pray about it, and ask God to strengthen you. With the help of the Holy Spirit and through the power of the Lord, pick yourself back up, and prepare to go back into battle with boldness!

Are there failures that you keep allowing to define you? Make a list today of the mistakes that are holding you back. Pray about them and ask God to help you turn those failures into future victories!

....

> Most powerful God, I bring my past failures before You. You know where I made mistakes; You know where I denied You and Your power. I ask for Your forgiveness. Now make me bold, dear Lord, and make my paths straight. Give me courage and wisdom to go into battle. In Jesus's name I pray! Amen!

REFRESH THE HEART

> For I have derived much joy and comfort from your love, my brother, because the hearts of the saints have been refreshed through you.
> —Philemon 1:7

Have you ever thought that you could actually refresh the heart of your customers, prospects, or your friends, neighbors, and coworkers? Philemon is a book in the Bible from which you rarely hear a sermon preached or a lesson taught. It's only one chapter with twenty-five verses. Now that's a book that's short enough that even I can read it! Contained within this book are lessons on forgiveness, unity, reconciliation, friendship, and kindness. But one key theme that Paul mentions several times is how Philemon refreshes his heart.

Philemon was most likely a successful businessperson and perhaps a local bishop. He was a well-respected community leader and considered to be very wealthy. In his letter to Philemon, Paul tells him the hearts of the saints have been refreshed because of you. Paul states this in verse 7, and it was important enough that he repeats it again in verse 20. Philemon was a partner with Paul in his ministry. He was someone Paul could count on, someone that he looked forward to seeing, and someone that brought joy to Paul. He refreshed Paul's heart.

So do your customers and the people you encounter daily look forward to seeing you? Think about that: In your role as a sales rep, you could actually refresh the heart of a client or coworker.

Each of us has a unique role. Being a sales rep presents the opportunity every day to show others that we come into contact with simple Christian principles. Basic principles like kindness, grace, mercy, forgiveness, empathy, compassion, sympathy, and love. We live in an era where political correctness can be a slippery slope and can make it extremely difficult to profess our Christian beliefs. We also live in a time that every sales transaction is becoming less and less personal. Regardless of the situation, we can still strive to be a positive influence to each person we encounter.

So how can we refresh our customer's hearts? A good place to start is to pray for them. Maybe you are not able to pray with them in person, but you can certainly send up a prayer for them before your meeting. Pray for them while you're waiting in your car in the parking lot. Pray for them before your call or after your meeting. Lift them up and ask God to bless them, provide for them, or protect them. Celebrate their accomplishments. Show empathy in their challenges. Be compassionate when they encounter trials. Show concern when they share details about their family. When the opportunity does present itself, pray with them, and let them know that you are praying for their business and their families. If you keep a customer long enough, you will walk through various stages of life with them. Along the way, take an interest in where they are in their life. Be genuinely interested in their activities, hobbies, and their lives.

The next time you set up a meeting with your client or prospective customers, pause and think about how your visit could refresh their hearts. When we take this kind of an approach, it moves our job from merely a way to make an income to a way to have a ministry. I think you will find that if you take the time to get to know your clients and, with genuine concern, really take an interest in them, you will be like Philemon was to Paul, a source of refreshment to their hearts.

Do your customers look forward to seeing you, or do they dread the meeting? What customers come to your mind that you could be refreshing to their hearts? What would you need to do in order to show more compassion for them?

....

> Gracious heavenly Father, I come before You today and ask You to help guide me, show me, and teach me where I can be compassionate to the people I encounter. Let me be a light to them. Let me be refreshing to their hearts. I give You the glory in Christ's name! Amen!

DON'T GIVE UP

> The seventh time around, when the priests sounded
> the trumpet blast, Joshua commanded the army,
> "Shout! For the LORD has given you the city!
> —Joshua 6:16

How many times have you made one sales call, you got turned down and then gave up? Perhaps you even made two, three, or even more and still gave up. When the Israelites came upon the gates of Jericho, they found the gates were securely locked. God said to Joshua, "See, I have delivered Jericho into your hands." God had promised Joshua they would conquer the city, but there was still work to do. There was still specific instruction that needed to be carried out. There was still effort that was required. God gave Joshua very detailed instructions. They were to march around the city seven times, and on the seventh time, the priests were to blow their trumpets and the army was to shout as loud as they could. Joshua 6:20 says, "When the trumpets sounded, the army shouted, and at the sound of the trumpet, when the men gave a loud shout, the wall collapsed; so everyone charged straight in, and they took the city." Amen! God is a conquering God!

How exciting would that be to march around your "blue whale" strategic target account, give a blow on the trumpet, and with a loud shout, the client is yours? According to Sales Enablement Report Statistics from Hub Spot, it takes an average of eighteen calls to actually connect with a buyer. Eighty percent of sales require five follow up calls. Forty-four percent of salespeople give up after one follow up call. Forty-eight percent of sales reps never make one follow-up call. Imagine that by simply making one follow-up call, you give yourself a better than 50 percent chance. That big sale, your Jericho, could be just one follow-up away. Just one extra phone call, one extra email away. In verse 21, it says they devoted the city to the Lord. Have you devoted your business to the Lord? I encourage you today; make that extra follow up call. Watch the Lord allow you to conquer your Jericho. Watch the Lord help you land that big account and dedicate it to the Lord!

> Lord, we pray today for our Jericho. We pray that You would help us conquer that fortified city. That account that appears to have the gates locked and the walls secure. We give You praise and honor for what You do in our lives and what we know You are going to do! We dedicate ourselves, our families, and our business to You, Lord! In Jesus's name we pray! Amen!

YOUR WAR CRY

> But Joshua had commanded the army, "Do not give a war cry, do not raise your voices, do not say a word until the day I tell you to shout. Then shout!"
> —Joshua 6:10

I can't tell you how many times I have heard about a salesperson going around telling everyone about a big deal they were going to close only to have that opportunity slip through their hands and lose it to a competitor. I once had a contractor that I worked with secure his largest sale in the history of his company by simply following up on a project he overheard another contractor talking about at a trade show. I recall a very large project that I lost by making a very rookie mistake. I took inaccurate information I was given about who was going to be awarded a certain contract and proceeded to talk with that contractor about the deal. I was already partnered up with another contractor but was trying to get additional information, and in the process, I completely alerted them. Come to find out, they were not even aware they were going to be included until I started talking. They ended up winning that project with one of my competitors. I learned a very tough lesson that day: Do not raise my voice or give away my position in a deal.

Joshua was preparing to conquer the city of Jericho. He told the army that he commanded, "Don't give a war cry or raise your voices until it's time to shout!" That's great advice we need to follow in our sales strategies. It's one thing to collaborate with trusted partners, advisors, or counterparts; but we need to be very careful about who we talk with about a deal before it's time to talk about it. There's an old saying, "Loose lips sink ships." It can be true in war, and it's true in the sales world as well. When we talk about our deal and the wrong person just happens to be listening, say goodbye to that commission check. Sometimes it's our arrogance doing the talking and our pride takes over about landing that big deal before it's actually closed. We should exercise caution on who, when, where, and how much we talk about an opportunity before it is 100 percent closed. Don't give out your war cry and alert the competition until the deal is done!

....

> Heavenly Father, thank You for caring about the details of our life. Help us to use restraint when we should exercise restraint. We recognize that our pride and selfish ambition can sometimes take over, and we want to tell everyone what we have accomplished. Help us to remain humble at all times. Amen!

PURPOSE IN YOUR HEART

> But Daniel purposed in his heart that he would not defile himself with the portion of the king's meat, nor with the wine which he drank: therefore he requested of the prince of the eunuchs that he might not defile himself.
> —Daniel 1:8

Daniel and his three friends, Shadrach, Mishael of Meshach, and Azariah of Abednego were brought into the king's palace to teach, learn, and serve the king of Babylon. They were to eat and drink what the king told them to eat. The only problem was that these three were children of Israel, and God had given them strict rules on what their dietary habits should be. To eat the food and drink the wine of the King would mean they would have to make a choice and go against what God had told them to do, and they would defile themselves and go against God's laws. In verse 8, it says Daniel purposed in his heart that he would not defile himself. He purposed, he resolved, he was determined. Daniel made up in his mind that he would not violate God's law. God honored these four and gave them wisdom, understanding, and skill. In verse 10, it says the king would reach out to them for counsel and there was none like them. In all matters, they were ten times smarter and skilled with wisdom and understanding. Ten times better and none like them!

So now the question comes to us: What have we purposed in our hearts? What are we determined in our hearts and in our minds to do or perhaps not do? In order not to defile ourselves before God, we must first know God. We must surrender to his will for our lives starting with accepting Jesus Christ as our personal Lord and Savior. Let him be Lord of your life and guide you in your life. God has given each one of us a conscience, that still, small inner voice. He has given us the ability to know and understand the difference between right and wrong. He has also given us His word, the Bible, to help guide us. When it comes to our business world, we must abide by the rules of your company, various state, local and national laws; and we must be determined to abide by God's rules for our lives. I often find in the heat of the battle, or when a big deal is on the line, it's easy to give in to the thought of compromise what you know you should do. It's especially challenging if we happen to find ourselves behind on our quota or way behind our sales target for the year. Perhaps the manager is really laying the pressure on you to close more business. If we have not purposed in our heart, if we have not determined what our moral compass is beforehand, we more than likely will succumb to the pressure of closely a deal. Perhaps compromising our own standards, God's standards and maybe even breaking a law. Let's be like Daniel, Shadrach, Meshack, and Abednego to be determined, be resolved, and purpose in our hearts to serve the Lord in every aspect of our lives including our sales career!

....

> Dear gracious heavenly Father, thank You for giving us the ability to determine right from wrong. Help us in our daily lives including my job, my family, with my friends, and in my sales. Help me to purpose in my own heart that I will serve You. Lord, let me be like Daniel and grant me wisdom and understanding that comes from You! Thank You, Lord! Amen!

PRAY FERVENTLY

> Elijah was a man with a nature like ours, and he prayed fervently that it might not rain, and for three years and six months it did not rain on the earth. Then he prayed again, and heaven gave rain, and the earth bore its fruit.
> —James 5:17–18

Do you have a list of things that you have been praying for, and it never seems to happen? In James 5, it says Elijah was a person just like you and me. He prayed for rain for three and a half years, and it never rained. Not even a drop, and it says he prayed fervently. I'm not so sure that I've ever prayed fervently, and I'm confident that I've never prayed consistently for that long. Oh, I've prayed for different things over the years and, in some cases, even fasted, prayed, wept, and probably even begged God for extended periods of time, but Elijah prayed all day every day for three and a half years, and nothing happened. Not even a drop of rain—not even a light mist or light dew. Nothing! But then it says he prayed again, and what happened! The heavens opened up, the earth bore its fruit, and it began to rain!

Elijah had faith the Lord would deliver. He never gave up, and God was faithful in answering his prayer. So here are some questions: Have you been praying fervently for your family, friends, neighbors, coworkers, clients, prospects, for your own business? Another word for *fervently* is *intensely* or *zeal*. Am I praying intensely with zeal and expectation the Lord will be faithful and answer? Is our prayer with the right intent? I once made a list of several key targets, and I begin to pray. I would pray every day specifically for the decision makers at those large accounts. Now I do not always subscribe to the prosperity gospel of materialism. I don't think the "name it and claim it" type of prayers are necessarily biblical, but I do know this: God delivered each and every one of those named accounts. I saw revenue come in for each one within a year's time. As I reflect back, it truly was amazing how God orchestrated the scenarios for each one of those clients. We serve an amazing God. Perhaps, like Elijah, you need to pray again. I want to encourage you to be fervent in your prayers. Pray for your prospects, your clients, your coworkers. Pray for the neighbors, your family, your friends. Be like Elijah, pray with zeal, pray intensely, and pray fervently!

> God of heaven and earth, we humbly come before You and ask for You to be faithful and deliver the prayers of our hearts, Lord. Let it be done for Your glory! Let us shout with praise as You open up heaven and let it rain on our lives! Thank You for what You are doing and what You are going to do! In the blessed name of Jesus we pray! Amen!

SEIZE THE DAY

> Now listen, you who say, "Today or tomorrow we will go to this or that city, spend a year there, carry on business and make money." Why, you do not even know what will happen tomorrow. What is your life? You are a mist that appears for a little while and then vanishes.
> —James 4:13–14

I have often been guilty of worrying, fretting, and generally working myself up into a panic just thinking about hitting a sales goal. I overthink or fear what might happen if I failed to hit the target. I think for myself, it's the competitive side of hating to lose, that overwhelming will to win and my desire to not fail that pushes me to levels that are beyond what God would want. It may be simply a fear of failure or maybe my self-worth has been measured by an accomplishment. Regardless, when we get our emotions so worked up thinking about making money or hitting sales goals, God calls that sin. Don't get me wrong; having a plan, a strategy and a goal is not a bad thing. After all, Proverbs 24:27 tells us to prepare our work outside, get everything ready for yourself in the field, and after that build your house. It speaks of preparation and planning. Where we run into the problem is when our arrogance takes over and our pride swells up, and we start talking about what we're going to do in the future with no regard to what God's plan may be for us, for our business, for our family, and for our lives.

What James is saying in these verses is speaking to our arrogance about what we're going to do tomorrow. Our pride in what we're going to do in the future. Boasting about making money. James 4:14 asks us, "Why are you talking about what you're going to do tomorrow?" Your life is like a mist or a vapor. Poof and it's gone. We are not promised one more second on this earth. We need to make the most out of each second. That is true in life and in business. Perhaps in the realm of business, it's making that call today to the prospect you've been thinking about. Maybe it's reaching back out to that client and thanking them for doing business with you. More importantly, how are we spending today glorifying the Lord? Let's be determined to make the most out of today. Proverbs 16:9 says, "In their hearts humans plan their course, but the LORD establishes their steps." Let's be about our Father's business today. If we are only promised this moment, then let's seize the day.

> Blessed Father and Redeemer, we humbly come before You and ask us to have clear focus. Lay before us the plans that You have for our lives, for our families, for our business. Bless the plans that I have for Your glory but Lord, establish my steps as I go about my day. Thank You, Lord, for loving me, caring for me, and providing for me. Put people in my path that mean good and remove the people that mean harm to my life. Make my path straight. I praise You in the name of Jesus. Amen!

SUPPLY CHAIN ISSUES AND FEEDING THE MULTITUDE

> They said to him, "We have only five loaves here and two fish." And He said, "Bring them here to me."
> —Matthew 14:17–18

The Bible records two separate instances where Jesus fed a multitude of people by using some fish and some bread. The feeding of the five thousand is the only miracle other than the resurrection that is recorded in all four gospels. In Matthew 15 and Mark 8, the Bible records another example when Jesus fed four thousand. In both cases, significant crowds had gathered, and as the day wore on, the disciples became concerned they didn't have food to feed the people. How would they feed all these people with only a few fish and a little bit of bread? The supply chain was stressed, broken, and was absolutely diminished. The situation looked bleak. The disciples may have been panicking, but they at least knew what to do: Bring the problem to Jesus. Matthew 14 records that a little boy had packed his lunch, and I love what Jesus said, "Bring them here to me."

As I write this, the current supply chain is absolutely disrupted. Products that you are accustomed to having readily available are on short supply and hard to find. The marketplace is seeing product constraints that has created a real delivery challenge. It becomes extremely painful and stressful to see opportunities slip away due to delivery issues or you lose a deal because your company may not be able to fill the order. As a sales rep, the hardest part of your job is supposed to be getting the purchase order, not the delivery. If you are a commission-based sales rep, seeing legitimate opportunities just vanish is frustrating. A successful sales rep is trained to close a deal and fight to the bitter end. We need to be just like the disciples and bring our situation to Jesus. Just like the little boy with the fish and bread, bring what you have to Jesus, and He can be in the multiplication business. It may appear there is no way my company can deliver the products, but Jesus says, "Bring it here to me." He can turn something that looks hopeless into excess. In both cases of feeding the multitude, it says they all ate and were satisfied. Not only were they satisfied, but the Bible also records they had more than enough and had leftovers. So much, they picked up twelve baskets of leftovers.

So do you find yourself in a situation that looks hopeless? Does it appear there's not enough product to go around? There is no way my orders are going to get filled? Well, I encourage you to bring it to Jesus. He is in the multiplication business.

> Jesus, we come before You today and say, "Help! My situation looks bleak, but I know if You are involved, You can turn a little into a lot." We give it to You, Lord, and ask for Your blessings on our work, on our family, on our business, on our friends, and on our circumstances. We give You praise for what You are going to do, and we thank You for taking care of our needs. In Jesus's name we pray! Amen!

SUPPLY AND DEMAND

> His mother said to the servants, "Do whatever he tells you."
> —John 2:5

The first recorded miracle that Jesus performed was at a wedding banquet when he turned water into wine. The story recorded in John says that Jesus was attending a wedding when the host ran out of wine. There was a supply-and-demand problem. Mary, Jesus's mother, didn't know how to fix the problem, but she knew exactly what to do. She immediately took the problem to Jesus. She goes on to tell the disciples, "Do whatever he tells you to do."

The term *logistics* is one that most people have come to understand as the supply chain has been strained. We've all seen stores with empty shelves. It's routine when a major snowstorm hits or a hurricane for stores to run out of bread, milk, or gas. For those of us that have been in sales, we completely understand supply and demand. You may run into situations where the demand for your product exceeds production or the opposite occurs, and you have more than enough product, but the demand is not there. In either case, our first response needs to be just like Mary's: Take it to Jesus and do whatever he says to do. Jesus is in the logistics business. He understands supply and demand. When God gets involved, He is able to not just add new business but multiply that business. If Jesus can turn water into wine, not only can He create demand, He also can solve the supply challenge.

....

> Jesus, help me today to lean completely on You for all my needs. Lord, if You can turn water into wine, You can solve my sales needs. Thank You for caring about the smallest details in my life!

VISION STATEMENT

> And the Lord answered me: "Write the vision, make it plain on tablets, so he may run who reads it. For still the vision awaits its appointed time; it hastens to the end-it will not lie. If it seems slow, wait for it; it will surely come; it will not delay.
> —Habakkuk 2:2–3

At the beginning of each year, most sales reps sit down and work through their business plan or develop their strategy for the year. You think through your accounts. Decide what you want to accomplish and start working on a plan. It is important to have an idea of what direction we are going. What should a good business plan include? Revenue targets, identified targets, strategies built around those targets, what you're hoping to accomplish for the year. These are all good attributes to a plan.

Habakkuk 2 says to write down that vision. Make it plain and post it where you can read it. Do you have a vision statement for yourself, for your family, for your business? I would suggest the very first thing we should do is start by asking the Lord, "What should be my vision?" and write it down. I once had a year when I lost my number 1 account. This customer represented a significant amount of revenue. I had no idea what I was going to do and how I was going to replace those sales. I prayed about it, and I really believe that God laid several new customers on my mind. I wrote the names of those accounts down and developed a plan around them. The accounts I listed were major global accounts. Customers that I had never done any business with. As I started working the plan and vision that God gave me, it took time. For months, it didn't seem like any progress was happening. In my mind, it seemed slow, but by the end of the year, revenue was generated with every one of those new accounts. In addition to replacing the revenue with brand-new accounts, I had regained the original account that I lost. God not only restored it, but He also multiplied it. If you make God a part of your vision statement and allow Him to help give you direction, it will surely happen!

....

> Lord, today I ask that You provide me with a vision for my business and for my family. Give me the strategies, the wisdom, and the plans—plans to prosper and make my business successful. Put customers on my mind and in my path. Praise be to You as I know this will happen!

GIVE ME SUCCESS

> O Lord, let your ear be attentive to the prayer of your servant, and to the prayer of your servants who delight to fear your name, and give success to your servant today, and grant him mercy in the sight of this man. "Now I was cupbearer to the king."
> —Nehemiah 1:11

Is it wrong to ask God to grant you success in your job? Nehemiah was to appear before the king to ask if he could go to his father's city of Jerusalem and repair the wall and the city that had fallen in ruins. This was the sort of request that if it went wrong could cost Nehemiah his life. Nehemiah was a servant; he was a cupbearer to the king. Nehemiah approached the king with a humble but bold confidence. He not only asked to be released from his duties so he could go do the work, but he also asked for letters from the king so he could pass through the country without being held up. A bold request. Keep in mind that during this time, servants were not to approach a king without the possibility of facing severe consequences and face the real potential of being put to death. Even if granted permission to travel to Jerusalem, Nehemiah would face a daunting task. He would have to travel over 800 miles, endure the people that were living in complete poverty, face constant mocking, and use up his personal resources. He would face tremendous opposition from several enemies trying to overtake Jerusalem. This was a major task. Was Nehemiah successful? Yes. The story tells us that not only did he repair the wall but he also completed it in fifty-two days. Keep in mind, this wall was over 2.5 miles long, 39 feet high, and 8 feet thick. This was a substantial project.

If God has placed you in the job or position that you are in, He does not want to see you fail. He wants to grant you success.

Nehemiah started with prayer; he prayed before he went before the king. He prayed for success, he prayed throughout the task, he prayed for protection, and he prayed every time he faced opposition. Are you facing a daunting task today? I would encourage you today to start with prayer. Ask God to grant you favor and to give you success. If you face opposition, stop and pray that God will grant you protection and keep you safe. And just like Nehemiah, God will grant you success, keep you from harm, and show you favor.

> Lord, I face a daunting task today. I come before You and ask You to grant me success! Show me favor. Put the people in my path that intend good and remove the people that want to bring harm. Let me be careful to always give You praise for all that You have done in my life. I thank You that You are a God that cares about the smallest details in my life. In Jesus's name I pray, amen.

BE A PERSON OF VALOR

And the angel of the Lord appeared to him and said to him, "The Lord is with you, O mighty man of valor."
—Judges 6:12

Valor is defined as great courage in the face of danger, especially in battle. Often in sales, we may be tempted to take the shortcut just to get ahead or to hit our numbers. We may tell a little lie just to close a deal. We may sneak a sale through or poach a deal from someone else's territory. When faced with adversity, pressure, or in the heat of battle, our character may be tested; and we are willing to compromise our standards. This often happens when we start feeling the pressure of hitting our quota or just the temptation to close that big deal.

Gideon's life may have been characterized as normal and maybe even fearful with feelings of being inadequate when the angel of the Lord spoke to him. As a matter of fact, he was pressing wheat out of fear in the winepress room when the angel appeared to him. I'm sure when the angel appeared and called him a mighty warrior, he may have even looked around to see who they were speaking to. Gideon would go on to lead Israel to victory over the Midianites in battle, but it all started with God speaking into Gideon's life and calling him a mighty warrior and Gideon fully surrendering and trusting the Lord. Gideon would fulfill this calling and be a man of valor.

God has called us in our positions and in our sales roles to be people of valor. This means doing what is right even when we face adversity. Standing strong when challenges come our way. Being courageous when we're pressed up against the wall. Displaying character when our sales quota is staring us in the face every morning. We should want our reputation as a professional sales representative to be one of courage, one of conviction, one that displays tremendous character and a person that does not compromise God's standards. We need to be people of valor!

....

> Lord, help me show courage in the face of trials today. God help me be a person of valor. Let me trust You for my provisions. Give me confidence that all things are possible with You. Go before me today. Put customers in my path that will be acceptable to my offerings. Guide my meetings. Grant me wisdom. Let me be a person of valor! In Jesus's name we pray! Amen!

ALL SCRIPTURE IS GOD-BREATHED

All scripture is breathed out by God and profitable for teaching, for reproof, for correction, and for training in righteousness, that the man of God may be complete, equipped for every good work.
—2 Timothy 3:16–17

We often think that when we are in sales, we live in this protective bubble where we have our personal life, our family life, our church life, then our business life exists outside of that, and all these lives shall never cross. We want to abide by one set of standards for our personal life and a different set of standards for our business life. Or we think the Bible was given to us only for telling us how to live within the confines of the church or our home. Second Timothy 3 tells us that all scripture is God-breathed. These verses tell us the Bible was given to us for teaching, equipping, and training for all areas of our life. So if the Bible was given to us for all aspects of our life, then it applies to our job as a salesperson as well. It applies to our business life. It applies to our meetings. It applies to our interaction with customers and coworkers. It applies to our sales calls. It applies to all aspects of our life. After all, if we call ourselves a Christ follower, our life should be an example for everyone to see something different. We should let them see the "Good News" that God has in store carried out in our daily lives. The Bible is filled with stories, examples, and tremendous truths that if we will look to them and follow them, they will help us not only in our daily personal lives but in our roles as sales professionals as well.

The Bible wasn't given to just preachers and Sunday school teachers to use to preach a sermon on Sunday morning, but it was given to us to equip us for every aspect of our lives. If God has placed you in your sales position, He wants you to succeed. The Bible is filled with great examples to follow, excellent guidelines and blueprint for success in all areas of our lives. As we open God's word, we will find biblical truths that will help guide us and direct us in negotiating with customers, working with vendors, and collaborating with our peers. Lessons on how to handle a difficult coworker or how to navigate a complex deal. When we put our trust in Him and we seek to live our lives by biblical truths, we can trust God to put the right customers in our path to help give us wisdom and insight on where to spend our time or handle a complex situation and provide guidance on how to help our business endeavors. It's all in God's holy word, the Bible!

> Lord, help guide me today in all aspects of my life. Show me and teach me the truths in Your Word that will help me be successful in my sales career. Put the customers in my path that will help me be productive. Remove the distractions from my life. Help me stay focused on You. I give You the praise, honor, and glory. In Jesus's name I pray. Amen!

LISTEN BEFORE SPEAKING!

If one gives an answer before he hears, it is his folly and shame.
—Proverbs 18:13

There is an old saying in sales that whoever does the most talking goes home with the product. In other words, as a sales rep, if you do all the talking and don't let the customer speak, they won't be buying your products or services. James 1:19 says we should be quick to hear and slow to speak. Taking the time to hear the customer can often be a difficult task for a sales rep. We are so quick to want to share our opinions, show the customer how smart we are, or start dumping products on the customer. Today's verse in Proverbs is saying if we start providing an answer before we listen to the customer, it is our folly or in other words it's foolishness.

Discovery is a key part of the sales process. Too many times, a sales rep wants to skip right past this crucial step and immediately dive straight into their presentation without ever listening to the customers' needs. We want to talk about what's important to us and not listen to the customers' needs. As a professional sales rep, we need to slow down and take time to discover what's important to the customer. Take the extra time to uncover their needs, understand their pain points, discover what's important to the client, and gain greater insight into where the point of entry may be with this customer. The discovery phase all begins with questions. Ask good questions, and let the customer do the talking without interrupting them. How do we ask good questions? Be sincere, take an honest interest in the other person's point of view, and give them time to answer. Listen to their needs and try to provide a valuable solution. Trust me, I have major attention issues, and I must really guard against my inclination to just blurt something out and immediately jump in as the customer is talking. I want to express my opinion and hit a major point as soon as they say a magical word or hit a hot topic. We just need to slow down and use the discovery phase, be inquisitive, ask questions, and be good listeners. I know this will serve us well in the sales process.

....

> Lord, help me be slow to speak and quick to listen. Remove the distractions and the temptation to talk too much and oversell. I trust You to put the right words in my mouth and the thoughts on my mind. I give You the honor, praise, and glory for all that You do in my life. In Jesus's name. Amen.

A NEW THING

> Remember not the former things, nor consider the
> things of old. Behold, I am doing a new thing; now
> it springs forth, do you not perceive it? I will make
> a way in the wilderness and rivers in the desert.
> —Isaiah 43:18–19

There's an old country song that says, "You got to know when to hold 'em and know when to fold them." Deciding it's time to move on from a customer or stop pursuing them may be one of the hardest decisions a sale rep has to make. Typically, by nature, we are just wired to compete. We like to win and get motivated by the thrill of the chase. After all, winning, closing deals, and meeting our sales budgets is what we are judged on as a sales rep. There are times that making the decision to stop trying to go after a client's business may be the right decision. After all, every minute that is spent with a client that is never going to buy from you is a second that you're not prospecting a new one. Now I know of stories where the sales cycle has taken months and even years. I've heard stories of sales reps that have called on prospective clients for years and made hundreds, if not thousands of sales calls on a specific client without any success and then suddenly land a massive purchase order that in the end did make it worthwhile. On the other hand, there may come a time that you must make a conscientious decision that I am going to spend my time prospecting for new opportunities.

Matthew 10:14 says to shake the dust off your feet and move on. If that time comes to move on from a customer, I suggest that you sit down with the customer, review the past sales history, discuss where you've been, and let them know in a professional manner that you are still available; but in order to be a good steward for your company and for your time, also let them know that you will be working with other prospects. You may find it amazing how the conversation may turn. I promise if you pray about it and make that decision, God will make a new way, or He may open that door in a whole different way.

I once had a top 25 Fortune 500 financial institution that I had called on for years without any success. Finally, one day, I met with the decision maker, and I walked through all the product sets that I had attempted to position and sell to them without any success. I let him know that I understand those items are off the table. Then I said, "What can we talk about?" To my amazement, he told me exactly what he was interested in; gave me the path to get the product approved, tested, and accepted; and how the purchase would transpire. This account that started as a six-figure purchase order generated over seven figures in the lifetime of the contract.

You may just be amazed that when you make the decision to move on, God decides to do a "new thing" and bring forth new life into that account. I was ready to move on, and God made a way in the wilderness. I encourage you to pray about it and ask God to point you in the right direction.

....

> Dear heavenly Father, there are customers that I have been trying to pursue, and I'm not sure what to do next. I ask You for guidance, direction, and to make the path clear. If you want me to move on, give me the wisdom to handle the conversation with professionalism. I put my trust in You and You alone to guide my steps! In Jesus's name I pray. Amen.

COUNT IT ALL JOY

Count it all joy, my brothers, when you meet trials of various kinds, for you know that the testing of your faith produces steadfastness. And let steadfastness have its full effect, that you may be perfect and complete, lacking in nothing.
—James 1:2–4

If you have spent more than a day in a sales role, you have probably experienced the jubilation of closing a deal and the discouragement from losing a sale you thought you had. I used to tell my bother-in-law who was a homicide detective and faced life-and-death situations every day that he didn't know stress; try having a sales quota hanging over your head, now that's stress. I was joking with him, of course, but for anyone that's experienced the highs and lows of the sale's emotional rollercoaster, you can relate. In my sales career, I have experienced losing my largest customer and having those feelings of time to get the resume brushed up only to have God come through in a big way. I once lost a top 50 Fortune 500 customer. It was by far my largest customer. It was devastating. In that year, God replaced that customer with not one but two Fortune 500 customers. A top 50 and a top 10 on that list. Just because God has a sense of humor, He also restored the original customer by the end of the year, and we did even more with them.

My sales friend, James, says to count it all joy when we face trials. Easier said than done, but I know that God is the ultimate provider when we fully trust Him. For me in the challenging times, God always lays two questions on my heart: Do you trust Me, and do you love Me? It always comes down to those two questions that I must resolve in my heart. James 1:5 says that if we lack wisdom, we should ask, and it will be given. I encourage you, if you are facing a trial today, if you are facing a real challenge, if you sense that fear is overtaking you, ask God to give you wisdom on how to handle the situation and count it all joy. Remember, 2 Timothy 1:7 says that God did not give us a spirit of fear but of power. Ask God today to meet you in this trial and go with confidence that He will come through; it will produce steadfastness and count it all joy, my sales friend.

....

> Jesus, I come before You today. Sometimes this sales role that I'm in creates an anxiousness that I know is not from You. Calm my fears. Let me truly count it all joy and lean only on You for my strength. Grant me wisdom to navigate through the sales storms. I trust You and I love You, Lord. In Jesus's name. Amen.

DON'T LET BITTERNESS TAKE ROOT

Let all bitterness and wrath and anger and clamor
and slander be put away from you along with malice.
Be kind to one another, tenderhearted, forgiving
one another, as God in Christ forgave you.
—Ephesians 4:31–32

There have been multiple times throughout my sales career where a peer has poached my territory for a sale, stole an account, or I've had situations where the company didn't want to pay the full commission. I have sales friends who have had their best accounts taken from them by their company and reassigned, costing them valuable commissions, and putting them in a personal financial bind. They laid all the hard groundwork with an account just to see a coworker rewarded for all their efforts. I've had accounts that I've worked hard to develop only to have another internal sales rep reap the benefits by swooping in. On more than one occasion, I had a sales rep from another region undercut my own pricing on an opportunity, stole the order, and cost the company a lot of money, only to end up being recognized as a rep of the year. It's real feelings and can cut deep into your emotions. These types of situations can create a real bitterness, and if allowed, they can take root in our hearts.

My wife can always tell when I've visited certain coffee shops or dined at a hibachi or fondu restaurant. That smell gets on my clothes, and it lingers until I can completely wash it out. That's the way bitterness can be. When it attacks you, it can linger and smell just like being sprayed by a skunk. It can render you helpless, immobilizing us, and our customers can detect that things are not right. It can hinder our future performance if we hold on to that grudge and bitter feelings. We must not let that bitterness take root or take hold in our life. Hebrews 12:15 says to not let bitterness take root because it causes trouble. In some situations, you may really need to consider changing companies. Especially if you're working for a morally corrupt culture at that company. In those circumstances, I would encourage you to pray and ask God to provide you with insight for that decision. In other situations, it's a matter of letting those bitter feelings go and moving on in our minds. You may say, but you don't know how deeply they cheated me or how much they hurt me. That may be true, but we can look no further than the cross at what Jesus did to find a model for forgiveness. Remember what Jesus said in Luke 23:34: "Father, forgive them for they know not what they do." Perhaps you have been someone that cheated a coworker. You've had those feelings of conviction that deep down you know you didn't do the right thing. I think in both cases, let's strive to be more like Jesus and seek forgiveness or if we've been done wrong, let's forgive them and move on. In the end, it will be freeing to your mind and ultimately help you excel in your next opportunity.

....

> Father, there have been circumstances in my past that I feel like I was done wrong. Help me to forgive and not allow bitterness to take root in my life. I thank You for being my provider. It's You that I depend on. Thank You for your forgiveness for my sins. Thank You for taking my place on the cross and paying my penalty. In Jesus's name I thank You and praise You. Amen.

REAP WHAT YOU SOW

Do not be deceived: God is not mocked, for whatever one sows, that will he also reap. For the one who sows to his own flesh will from the flesh reap corruption, but the one who sows to the Spirit will from the Spirit reap eternal life. And let us not grow weary of doing good, for in due season we will reap, if we do not give up.
—Galatians 6:7–10

The Bible is clear that we reap what we sow. The same can be said in sales; we also reap what we sow. You have often heard that "activities equal results" or "practice makes perfect." I would suggest this saying should be modified to say "good activities equal results" or "perfect practice makes you perfect." If you practice the wrong technique in a sport or playing a musical instrument, you will never perfect the right way to play. It is the same in sales, if you are not regularly generating revenue-producing activities, you will not see the results that you are hoping for. You may go through seasons where you slack off for a few days or maybe even weeks and your sales don't seem to suffer, but it will eventually catch up with you and your pipeline or sales revenue with begin to decrease.

A system that I used to ensure a steady flow of activities on a daily basis is what I call my "have a good day" formula. It's all based on assigning points for activities. I assign points every day to revenue-producing activities such as setting appointments, attending sales calls, prospecting, follow-up calls, networking, and customer visits. You can customize this formula or method to whatever industry you are in. I set a point value to each activity and must achieve a minimum number of points every day. Notice that I do not include getting a purchase order or closing a sale in my point system. The sale is the by-product of performing solid, revenue-generating activities.

Having used this system for many years, it's like clockwork: If I generate the minimum points every day, my sales funnel stays full, and the results will come. If I try to cheat my system, skip days, or just not generate the activities, it always shows up in my sales. As with any sales process, sometimes you may not see the immediate results, but just like Galatians says, don't grow weary of doing good, for in due season, you will reap the harvest. If you don't give up. Don't give up! Keep sowing the seeds, and you will reap the benefits.

> Lord, we know the seeds that You want us sowing is furthering your kingdom and helping lead others to Christ. We know that and acknowledge that. I come before You and ask that You help strengthen us and keep us from growing weary. Help me in my daily activities. Help me to not give up and to keep sowing those good seeds. I give You the glory, and we know that all good things are a gift from you. Thank you, Jesus. Amen!

POSITIVE GROWTH MINDSET

> Finally, brothers, whatever is true, whatever is honorable, whatever is just, whatever is pure, whatever is lovely, whatever is commendable, if there is any excellence, if there is anything worthy of praise, think about these things.
> —Philippians 4:8

How important is having a positive mindset to your success as a sales rep? Ask any sales consultant, and they will say that having a positive mindset is one of the major keys to having a successful career in a sales role. Psychology shows that your mindset dictates your emotions, which, in turn, influences the type of actions you take. In other words, if you stay positive, you're more likely to keep pursuing the activities that will generate results. Maintaining a positive, healthy mindset can be tough; after all, even the most successful sales reps are fortunate if they have a closing ratio that is greater than 10 percent. You must be prepared for rejection and thrive on the wins. A successful sales rep knows how to challenge that negativity and turn it into a positive. A famous basketball coach was once quoted as saying, "We're never losing. We're either winning or we're learning."

What are the characteristics of a positive mindset? They are enthusiastic, optimistic, adaptive, persistent, motivated, empathetic, honest, confident, passionate, responsible, focused, friendly, patient, creative, professional, and positive to name a few. That's quite a list. How do we maintain this mindset? Philippians tells us to think about things that are true, honorable, pure, and lovely. Think about things that are excellent and praiseworthy. A good way to maintain a positive mindset is to spend time with the Lord in prayer and meditating on His word and His goodness. Colossians 3 tells us to set our minds on things that are above, to put on love and to let the word of Christ dwell in us.

My sales friends, we all know that customers like to buy from people they like. The characteristics that are attractive to others are filled with having a positive mindset. First Corinthians 13 says that love is patient and love is kind. A positive mindset starts with love; it starts with our relationship with the Lord. After all, God is love, and God loves you.

> Jesus, we thank You that You are the complete definition of love. We thank You for working in us and helping us to have a positive mindset. Help us get rid of any negativity, thoughts, or emotions that are hindering our performance. Let us put on Your love every day. We give You honor, praise, and glory today. In Jesus's name. Amen.

USE YOUR RESOURCES

> I hope in the Lord Jesus to send Timothy to you soon, so that I too may be cheered by news of you. For I have no one like him, who will be genuinely concerned for your welfare.
> —Philippians 2:19–20

Paul had served as a mentor to Timothy. He first met Timothy in Lystra where Timothy lived along with his grandmother Eunice and his mother Lois. He had trained with Paul and traveled with him along with Silas on their quest to spread the gospel on their first missionary journey. Paul had sent Timothy to Corinth in the past on another mission trip and now was planning to send him to Philippi. Paul knows Timothy's character and his capabilities, and he feels completely confident to send him to Philippi and help minister to them. Paul recognized that Timothy was a man of God and was up for the task to travel to Philippi and carry out the mission.

Sometimes in our sales roles, we want to walk the path alone. Instead of utilizing available company resources, we choose to continue to call on the prospective customer over and over and deliver the same message and keep getting the same result. This can be for a variety of reasons. Perhaps we don't trust anyone else with our customer or maybe it's our pride of wanting all the credit for ourselves. Only 2 percent of sales happen during the first point of contact. Most sales require multiple follow-up contacts, and according to LinkedIn, statistics show that 80 percent of most sales require at least five follow-up calls to be successful. I once had a customer that I had called on for several years. I was only getting a portion of their overall business but continued to meet with them by myself. After talking with a business associate of mine, he recommended that I bring in our global sales engineer to meet with them with the hopes they could convince them to give us an opportunity to earn the piece of business that we had been missing. I had lived for a long time thinking just be grateful for what we are getting and not push the chance that we could lose it all. Bringing in a new and extremely capable resource that could deliver a powerful, persuasive message proved to be a magical formula. It turned out to be a very successful strategy and more than doubled the size of the account.

Paul realized that Timothy could be a great value and used him multiple times to help, encourage, and minister to others. I encourage you to look at your available resources and see who you can utilize to help you close or secure more business.

> Lord, thank You for giving me the knowledge and wisdom to consider other resources that can help me. Keep me from being arrogant and prideful in such a way that it hurts my business. Thank You for always providing, always caring, and always loving me! We look to You for all our provisions. In Jesus's name. Amen.

COMPASSION IS CONTAGIOUS

Jesus wept.

—John 11:35

As a kid growing up in Sunday school, anytime I was asked to recite a verse, John 11:35 was my go-to verse: "Jesus wept." Short, sweet, to the point, and the best part, easy to remember. At first glance, it seems like there's not much to the shortest verse in the Bible, but when you look closer, there's a lot packed into those words. In two little words, Jesus displays compassion, concern, empathy, sympathy, emotion, and ultimately, He will display His divine power. The story finds Jesus visiting his friends Martha, Mary, and their brother Lazarus who had become ill. Upon arrival, Jesus is informed that Lazarus had died three days earlier. Now obviously, Jesus is all-knowing, and this did not come as a surprise to Him but in this instance, Jesus was able to show empathy to His friends by mourning with them. Little did they know, Jesus would perform a divine miracle and bring Lazarus back from the dead, but in this immediate instance, He was able to show them compassion, weep with them, and provide comfort at an emotional time for them.

Compassion is a contagious emotion. Customers appreciate that you can identify with them and show care and concern for what they may be going through. When you're able to show concern for their situation, it not only helps you develop a deeper relationship, it also is one way that we can be a light to them and show them Christ in a loving way. Sometime in sales, the less we say, the better off we are. We are probably all familiar with the old phrase "Action speaks louder than words" or "underpromise and overdeliver." That could not be truer in this case of Jesus and Lazarus; His actions spoke volumes over the words. This is often the case in our sales roles. Our actions can speak volumes over what we say. I once had a prospective customer that had a heart attack. I knew him well enough that I decided to go visit him in the hospital. Upon arrival, I think he was a little surprised, but I could tell he was very appreciative of this sign of concern for him and his health. I was able to meet his wife, pray with him, and really show him some genuine compassion. Now I'm not advocating hanging out at the nearest emergency room and looking for prospective new clients, but I am recommending that if we will slow down and take the time, opportunities to show your customers compassion will present themselves. It doesn't even have to be a near-death experience but simply showing concern about the stress of their jobs, position, and decisions they must make will deeper your relationship with them. Genuine concern is the key and letting our motives be pure not just what we can get out of it. Customers will see right through that. It must come from the heart. I think you will find that showing customers concern and compassion is contagious and will endear them to you.

> Jesus, thank You for providing the ultimate example of compassion by taking our place on the cross. We love You and thank You for all that You do in our lives. Help us to be observant for opportunities to show compassion and concern. Let our motives be pure and about that person and not what we can get out of it. In Jesus's name, Amen.

ASK, SEEK, AND KNOCK

Ask, and it will be given to you, seek, and you will find; knock and it will be opened to you. For everyone who asks receives, and the one who seeks finds, and to the one who knocks it will be opened.
—Matthew 7:7–8

Ask, *seek*, and *knock*: These three words serve as a pattern for how we should approach God and our life. We first must come to the Lord and ask Him for guidance. We do this by asking God to forgive us and come into our life. We seek the answers through God's word, staying close to Him, and listening for His answers. And we knock to ask God to come into our hearts and align our thoughts with what He wants to accomplish in our life. If we keep this pattern, John 14:13 says, "If you ask anything in My name, it will be done." It's all about our motives in our requests and God's plan for our lives. Notice that *ask*, *seek*, and *knock* are proactive words? They are not passive; they are words of action. The day that we accept Jesus into our heart, His love is complete. We can't earn His favor, but we should continually be pursuing to be more like Christ in our daily lives.

The same proactive pursuit should be part of our daily sale lives. Mike Weinberg, a sales consultant and author says, "There's only three sales verbs that matter; create, advance, and close." Eighty-plus percent of your work week should be focused on these three verbs. I like to use what I call the 3, 2, 1 strategy: (3) Create new opportunities, advance the sales cycle, and close more deals. (2) Sell more. If you wake up in the morning and don't know what to do, sell more. And (1) win! Ultimately, that's what sales are all about—winning.

Be proactive in your pursuit of new business. Consider these statistics according to a study by Notta. Top salespeople spend an average of five hours per week on prospecting activities; 48 percent of salespersons never attempt follow-up calls, but 80 percent of sales require at least five follow-up calls to be successful. You can do the math. We must be proactive and remain proactive!

....

> Lord, You have given us a pattern to pursue You. Let my pursuit of You always be the main priority in my life. You have placed me in this position, and I depend upon You to put the right customers in my path, give me the knowledge to clearly communicate to them and the perseverance to stay consistent. Show favor to my actions, Lord! In Jesus's name I pray. Amen.

PERSEVERE THROUGH THE TRIALS

> Three times I was beaten with rods. Once I was stoned. Three times I was shipwrecked; a night and a day I was adrift at sea; on frequent journeys, in danger from my own people, danger from the Gentiles, danger in the city, danger in the wilderness, danger at sea danger from false brothers; in toil and hardship, through many a sleepless night, in hunger and thirst, often without food, in cold and exposure. And, apart from other things, there is the daily pressure on me of my anxiety for all the churches.
> —2 Corinthians 11:25–28

Paul is the very definition of perseverance. He was shipwrecked, beaten, hungry, cold, sleepless nights, lost at sea, and faced dangers everywhere he turned. On top of that, he was thrown in prison, had poor eyesight, and faced daily pressures, anxiety, and worry for the churches. Yet he continued pressing on. In 2 Timothy 4:7, he said, "I have fought the good fight, I have finished the race, I have kept the faith." Paul finished well. I think Paul could have made a good sales rep. He had the tenacity to overcome any obstacle thrown his way.

Sales can be hard. You face rejection, competition, and the constant disconnect that seems to always exist between sales and operations. You have supply chain issues, pricing restrictions, increased margin demands, and customer service challenges. You face the constant pressure of newer competitive products, other reps that seem to have endless energy, and the ever-increasing annual quota from corporate all while receiving typically very little praise. The pressures to continue to grow your business and hit plan never seem to go away all while trying to maintain a healthy work, life, family balance. It takes a special skill and discipline to stay on task, focused, and keep from losing it daily. Paul knew the secret to perseverance when he said in Philippians 4:12–13, "I know what it is to be in need, and I know what it is to have plenty." I have learned the secret of being content in any and every situation, whether well-fed or hungry, whether living in plenty of in want. I can do all things through him who gives me strength.

Soldier on, sales rep. Keep running the race and fighting the good fight. You've got this!

....

> Dear heavenly Father, some days it requires more strength than I think I have. It's on those days and every day that I turn to You as my provider, my shelter, my strength, and my Lord. Help me to maintain the fight. Help me to labor on. I pray in Your precious name of Jesus. Amen.

DEAD BONES CAN COME BACK TO LIFE

> So, Elisha died, and they buried him. Now bands of Moabites used to invade the land in the spring of the year. And as a man was being buried, behold, a marauding band was seen and the man was thrown into the grave of Elisha, and as soon as the man touched the bones of Elisha, he revived and stood on his feet.
> —2 Kings 13:20–21

Can you imagine being so filled with God's spirit and power that even when you're dead, you can have an impact on someone. Elisha was a prophet, miracle worker, and a disciple and protégé of Elijah. Second Kings 2:10 says that Elisha received a double portion of power when Elijah was taken away in a whirlwind. God had chosen Elisha to take Elijah's place in power and as a leader of the prophets. God used Elisha to minister, and he would go on to perform twice as many miracles as Elijah. In the verses today, we find the story of about a man who was dead; they were burying him, and in a haste, they just threw his body into the grave where Elisha had been buried. Can you even imagine the look on their faces when as soon as his body touched Elisha's bones, he was revived and just stood up. That's amazing power. Through the grace of God and the blood of Jesus, we have resurrection power.

Perhaps you have accounts that feel like that dead man that was thrown into the grave. Accounts that are dried up, opportunities that seem like they have hit a dead end, prospects that are just unresponsive and not progressing. Do you believe that God can bring those accounts back to life? Do you believe He can breathe new life back into old customers? We serve the same God that brought the dead man back to life by just touching Elisha's bones. Through the grace of God, we serve a risen Savior that conquered death and given us the promise of eternal hope and life. Ephesians 1:15–23 tells us that the same power that the Father used to raise Jesus from the dead is at work in us. I suggest you print the logos of your accounts or names of your prospects or customer list and put it in a visible place where you can see it every day. Pray for it every day. Ask God to use that same power that he used to raise the dead to breathe life into your accounts. Bring them back to life. Put air back into those dead prospects. Watch God's amazing power work through you and in them to bring them to life and give God the glory for what he has done!

....

> God, I believe that You are the God with resurrection power. I ask that You breathe life into my accounts. I ask that You restore old customers. I ask that You pour Your mighty power over my prospects. Let me see Your work in my life and in my business. I love You, Lord, and give You all the glory, praise, and honor for what You are doing! In Jesus's name. Amen.

MAKE A MEMORIAL

And Joshua said to them, "Pass on before the ark of the Lord your God into the midst of the Jordan and take up each of you a stone upon his shoulder, according to the number of the tribes of the people of Israel, that this may be a sign among you. When your children ask in time to come 'What do those stones mean to you?' then you shall tell them that the waters of the Jorden were cut off before the ark of the covenant of the Lord. When it passed over the Jordan, the waters of the Jordan were cut off. So, these stones shall be to the people of Israel a memorial forever."
—Joshua 4:5–7

It is important to remember what God has done in your life and make a marker to remember His faithfulness. The twelve tribes of Israel had faced many challenges on their journey to the promised land. They had wandered in the wilderness for forty years, saw God provide a way across the Red Sea with the enemy bearing down on them. They faced many hardships and challenges along the way and their leader, Moses died before entering this new land. Joshua, God's chosen replacement for Moses now stood at the banks of the Jordan River as they finally prepared to cross. They would once again need to see God's mighty hand in helping them find a way across the river. Keep in mind, this was not just walking through a little stream, but the Bible says the banks of the river were overflowing. Just as God had provided for them throughout their journey and just as God had provided a way across the Red Sea, He was once again faithful in providing a way across the Jordan. Joshua 3:17 says all of Israel passed over on dry ground. God told Joshua to have a leader from the twelve tribes carry a stone from the dry river, and they would make a memorial in remembrance of God's faithfulness and God's covenant with the people of Israel. So when they reached the other side, Joshua 4:20–24 says they took the twelve stones and make a marker and so all the future generations would know that Israel passed over the Jordan on dry ground. This marker would be significant as they prepared to battle to take the land God had promised them. It would serve as a reminder of God's faithfulness. They would look to that marker and remember how God had provided and delivered them.

It's important in all aspects of our life to remember how God has protected us and how God has provided. No doubt in your career and in your life, you can look back and recall specific times when God was faithful. I'm sure you can recall a time that it felt like there's no way I could survive this situation and God provided a way. Perhaps you're at a point in your career, with your job, or with your family where it just seems like there's no possible way that God can help. Maybe you're facing your own Jordan River. The water is just too deep, and there feels like no way it's going to work out. I encourage you to make a list, take it to God in prayer, let it go, and watch Him work. He is faithful. Make a marker in your life when you clearly see God come through. Perhaps it's a mental picture of God's faithfulness or maybe it's an actual memorial that you must remind yourself of just how God worked things out. Every time you look at it, you will be reminded that God protected me. Just like the people crossing the river, you will face another battle, and it will be important to look back and recall God's provisions and how it worked it out for you before.

> Lord, thank You for being a God that cares about me. Thank You for always providing a way. I come to You today and ask for Your protection, Your provisions, and Your direction in my life. Let me always remember how You have made a way for me. In Jesus's name I pray. Amen.

POWER OF A STORY

> Listen! Behold, a Sower went out to sow. And as he sowed, some seed fell along the path, and the birds came and devoured it. Other seeds fell on rocky ground, where it did not have much soil, and immediately it sprang up, since it had no depth of soil. And when the sun rose, it was scorched, and since it had no root, it withered away. Other seeds fell among thorns, and the thorns grew up and choked it, and it yielded no grain. And other seeds fell into good soil and produce grain, growing up and increasing and yielding thirtyfold and sixtyfold and a hundredfold.
> —Mark 4:3–8

Jesus told over thirty parables in the Bible. He loved to use stories that were simple and easy to understand to get his point across. Telling stories or parables was central to Jesus's life and the way He ministered. Using stories allowed Jesus to build rapport, gain trust and make it easier for the listener to understand the life lesson that was being taught. He would use stories to reveal the truth.

This is a great lesson for us in our sales roles and for our meetings and presentations. We need to have our stories prepared as well. Be ready to use examples to relay the thought that we are trying to explain. Have real life success stories that are relatable to the discussion. Know the story of our company or the reason for our product's existence. Have real-life examples of the application and the benefits that customers received. According to a Gartner study, 70 percent of executive buyers believe that customer stories are the best way to differentiate a company from its competitors. Stories are up to twenty-two times more memorable than just typical facts and figures.

The parable of the Sower in Mark 4 is the first recorded story that Jesus told in the book of Mark. At this time, agriculture would have been something the listeners could relate to. Jesus uses the examples of seed falling beside a road or on rocky ground to explain how some people will hear the gospel message but not respond but the seed that falls on good fertile soil will not only grow, but it will thrive. In Mark 4:20, Jesus says the ones that were sown on the good soil are the ones who hear the word and accept it and bear fruit.

Let us use stories to get our point across, but more importantly, let us be not only hearers of the word but doers as well.

> Jesus, thank You that you provided an example of how to communicate by using stories. Let us take this lesson and apply it to our own sales roles. Thank You for not only helping us plant in fertile soil but You provide the seeds and the rain to water those seeds. Let our stories fall on fertile ground. In Jesus's name. Amen!

ASK MORE QUESTIONS

> He said to them, "But who do you say that I am?" Simon Peter replied, "you are the Christ, the Son of the Living God."
> —Matthew 16:15–16

Jesus asked a lot of questions. There are over 307 questions that Jesus asks in the Bible. In almost every encounter, Jesus starts by asking questions or he finishes the conversation by asking questions and has a call to action. He used questions to help influence people and challenge their way of thinking. He used questions to reveal their hearts and make a difference in their lives. Jesus, being omniscient, already knew the answers before he ever asked, but by using well-thought-out, probing questions, he would be able to get the other person to start talking and lead them to start thinking about their answers.

Isn't it interesting in our sales meetings if we just ask more questions, we can build more rapport? If we can get the customer to start talking, they will lead us to what is most important to them, and it will allow us to uncover their true objections. Too many times, we want to rush right through discovery questions and hit the customer with what we want to present. We need to be prepared to ask more questions and spend more time in the discovery phase.

In the verses in Matthew 16, Jesus asks the disciples who people are saying the Son of Man is. They say some think John the Baptist, some say Elijah, and others say Jeremiah. That's when Jesus asks Peter one of the most important and direct questions, "But who do you say I am?" The way we answer that question today is the most important question we can answer. Who do you say Jesus is? Who is Jesus to you? Is he just a good teacher, a prophet, some mythical character in an old book, or is He the Messiah, the Risen Savior. Is he as Peter said, "Christ the Son of the Living God."

That's my prayer for you today. Yes, ask probing questions; yes, spend time asking discovery questions. Yes, get your customers to talking but in your own life; answer the most important question, and that is, who is Jesus to you?

....

> Jesus, thank You that we can truly know that you are Christ, the Son of the Living God. Thank You for loving us, thank You for caring for us, and thank You for being our Lord and Savior! Thank You, Jesus. In your precious name we pray. Amen.

WHEN WE ARE WEAK, HE IS STRONG

Three times I pleaded with the Lord about this, that it should leave me. But he said to me, "my grace is sufficient for you, for my power is made perfect in weakness." Therefore, I will boast all the more gladly of my weaknesses, so that the power of Christ may rest upon me. For the sake of Christ, then, I am content with my weaknesses, insults, hardships, persecutions, and calamities. For when I am weak, then I am strong.
—2 Corinthians 12:9–10

Aren't you glad that when you are tired, weak, and powerless, Christ is strong and still at work? As I write this, I am finishing up a week of national sales meetings, along with a tradeshow, and the national conference for our industry. This is a week that includes numerous meetings, presentations, dinners with customers, and constant conversations along with just being completely out of my normal sleep, workout, and dietary routines. I am exhausted, and my mind is tired.

It is comforting to know that even when we feel like we don't have another ounce of energy or effort left in us, that God is still at work. As a matter of fact, Paul tells us in 2 Corinthians that when we are weak, the power of Christ may rest upon us. His grace is sufficient for us. That means if we have prayed and living for Christ, God is at work, moving, orchestrating, maneuvering, and helping us. That thought alone should put a little extra air in our lungs. We have a great provider that cares about us that is always at work. Hebrews 4 tells us that we enter His rest when we believe in Him. The rest that Hebrews mentions is as believers we have comfort in knowing that we have been sanctified through the cross of Jesus. But we can also have confidence that we can enter the rest that God provides even when we are weak and tired. Now that is something worth getting excited about.

....

> Jesus, thank You that You have promised to be working for us even when we are tired and weak. I ask that You lead, guide, and direct my path. Let me find peace, rest, and refresh my mind and my thoughts. I give You the praise for what You are doing on my behalf. Show me favor today. In Jesus's name I pray. Amen.

FINISH STRONG

> I have fought the good fight, I have finished
> the race, I have kept the faith.
> —2 Timothy 4:7

Have you ever known someone that quit working years before they retired? In the air force, we called it the road program, retired on active duty. In other words, you're still getting paid, but the effort is no longer there. I've worked with individuals that have basically mailed it in for several years without putting forth any real effort. They're in essence stealing from the company. Many times, it's individuals that land in a role that doesn't have a lot of accountabilities, or they've put it on cruise control and just doing the bare minimum to get by.

Paul tells us in 2 Timothy that he fought the good fight, he finished the race, and he kept the faith. Paul had been beaten, thrown in jail, shipwrecked, falsely accused, but he fought till the very end and never gave up. That should serve as encouragement for us as well. Perhaps you're coming to the end of your career, and it's tempting to start to throttle back, put in less effort, and just do enough to stay off the radar. As Paul instructed us, resist that temptation. Finish strong and fight till the very end. As Christ followers, we should serve as an example to others. Let our yes be yes and no be no, and let our work efforts reflect the work ethic that God would expect.

The same could be said when we're in our prime, and we're in the middle of chasing an opportunity. I can't tell you how many times I've chased an opportunity for months then give up and quit trying, only to find afterward that if I had just kept trying for a little longer, it would have paid off. That's a gut punch. It always stings when you find out how close to the finish line you were after the fact.

So let's be like Paul said and fight the good fight, finish strong, and keep the faith.

....

> Dear heavenly Father, You have told us to keep fighting, stay strong, keep in the race, and finish what we have started. Help give us the endurance, strength, and will power to fight that good fight. We will be careful to give You the praise for what You are accomplishing. Thank You, Jesus, for being a Savior who cares. I love You, Lord. Amen.

GOD DIRECTS OUR PATH

And they went through the region of Phrygia and Galatia, having been forbidden by the Holy Spirit to speak the word in Asia. And when they had come to Mysia, they attempted to go into Bithynia, but the Spirit of Jesus did not allow them. So, passing by Mysia, they went down to Troas. And a vision appeared to Paul in the night: a man of Macedonia was standing there, urging him, and saying, "Come over to Macedonia and help us."

—Acts 16:6–9

Paul had a plan and strategy that he would go to Asia, preach the word, and spread the gospel to that region. God had another plan. Through a vision lay, it would be put on Paul's heart to go to Macedonia instead. What a great thing that Paul responded to that change in direction. Paul would go on to meet Lydia who would accept Christ and start the first house church in that area. Paul and Silas would be thrown in prison, but through this experience, the Philippian jailer would come to know Christ along with his entire family. Through this obedience and change, the gospel would eventually spread throughout the entire Roman territory.

The Bible tells us we should have a plan, a vision, and a strategy but we need to be flexible and nimble to respond when God points us in a different direction. Perhaps you are sensing the doors are closing on the accounts, the customers, or the direction that you have in mind. Psalm 46:10 says, "Be still and know that I am God. I will be exalted among the nations; I will be exalted in the earth!" If you are sensing the path that you're on is coming to an end or there's no movement, I encourage you to be still and listen for God's direction. He may be putting a new plan in place and placing a new direction on your heart. Henry Blackaby in the Bible study *Experiencing God* says to find out where God is working and move to where He is. Get real quite with the Lord, spend some alone time with Him, listen for his voice, and watch for His direction. He may have a new strategy and plan that He's trying to tell you.

....

> God, thank You for caring about the smallest details in my life. I love You and appreciate all that You do. All good gifts come from You. Lead me, guide me, and direct my life. Make the path so bright that I can tell it's only from You. Thank You, Jesus, for loving me. Amen.

SELFISH AMBITION

> Do nothing from selfish ambition or conceit, but in humility count others more significant than yourselves. Let each of you look not only to his own interests, but also to the interests of others.
> —Philippians 2:3–4

Have you ever had someone that you feel like you're constantly in competition against them? It may be a coworker, a competitor from another company, a neighbor, or perhaps even a sibling or family member. I have a friend that has a sales rep peer in the same company that he seems to be always up against for various awards. It has come down to the wire several times between the two of them for sales rep of the year. They seem to always be competing for who gets to go on the annual presidents' trip for the top performer. They have adjacent regions, so they are constantly competing against each other and in some cases for the same opportunities. Their kids even competed against each other for the company college scholarship. My friend has come out on the losing side of that grudge match on more than one occasion. It would be easy to let the seeds of jealousy or envy take root. After all, most successful sales reps are competitive by nature. They hate to lose and that may override their desire to win, and there is a difference between the two. Top-performing sales reps are typically always competitive, striving to be the best, they like to have their accomplishments acknowledged, and they hate to be on the losing side of anything. When we win it is easy to let selfish ambition, conceit, and arrogance set it. If we lose, bitterness, envy, and resentment can find its way into our thoughts.

Philippians tell us that we are to count others more significant than ourselves. In everything we do, we should be humble and do it without selfish ambition. Proverbs 16:18 says that pride comes before destruction. If we win, we should remain humble. If we lose, we should remain humble. There is a difference between being proud of an accomplishment and being prideful. This is not to say that we should lack confidence. Quite the contrary. As a successful sales rep, there should always be a certain sense of self-confidence. As believers, we should display humble confidence in our sales professions, in our abilities that God has given to us and in our accomplishments. But our personal value and our self-worth should not simply be placed on whether we win a sales award or whether we lose one. As Christ followers, let our value be determined by the Lord. Isaiah 43:4 says, "You are precious in my eyes and honored, and I love you, I give men in return for you, people in exchange for your life." Let our lives be a display of God's love and represent a humble confidence.

> Our Father in heaven, let my life always be an indication of Your love for me and You working in and through me. Let me remain humble in any accomplishment. Let me display humble confidence and remove any roots of arrogance, bitterness, jealousy, envy, or pride. It's because of You that I have been given my abilities. Let me be careful to always give You praise in any accomplishment. Thank You, Lord! Amen.

LET IT RAIN

And he said to his servant, "Go up now, look toward the sea." And he went up and looked and said, "There is nothing." And he said, "Go again," seven times. And at the seventh time he said, "Behold, a little cloud like a man's hand is rising from the seas."
—1 Kings 18:43–44

Do you feel like you have been experiencing a drought in your career, your sales, or perhaps your life? James 5:17–18 says, "Elijah was a man with a nature like ours, and he prayed fervently that it might not rain, and for three years and six months it did not rain on the earth. Then he prayed again, and heaven gave rain, and the earth bore fruit." This story in the book of James retells a story that appears in 1 Kings 17 and 18 where Elijah predicted a drought and for three and a half years, it did not rain. But in 1 Kings 18:45, it says after praying, the heavens grew black with clouds and wind, and there was a great rain. You may be experiencing what you feel like has been a long drought. Perhaps your sales pipeline has dried up, there's no prospect of a sale anywhere in sight, your quota is looming over your head, and there's no sign of any deals coming your way. It may even feel like the Lord is just not listening to your prayers. Don't lose hope, and don't get discouraged. I don't know how God plans to answer your prayer, but I know that God is working on your behalf. It may not appear there's any sign of relief, the sales prospects are dried up, the clouds may be hanging over your head but not producing the rain necessary to make the conditions right to produce fruit. God is at work even when you can't see it or feel it.

In Daniel 10:12–14, it says that Daniel prayed, and his prayer was heard, but it took twenty-one days for the angel Michael to arrive to provide help and an answer. My sales friend, don't lose hope. God is at work, and He cares about you.

So what do you do while you're waiting to see the results? Just like Elijah, pray, pray again, and pray again. Keep praying until you have your answer. Take a deep breath and review where you're at. Take an assessment of the situation. It may not be as bad as you think. Your emotions may be overloaded, misfiring, and leading your thoughts down a harmful path. Call your best customers. I find in seasons of drought. If I call on my very best clients, it often helps to get my mindset right again. It helps to remind you that you have a good product, you are a trusted advisor, and your customers appreciate you and your product. It may provide additional affirmation, and that's all that's needed to give you the confidence to give it another try with new prospects. Go back over your prospect list and rethink your strategies. Review what you've already said and perhaps you need to tweak your messaging. Go back to the discovery phase. In some cases, it's just a matter of asking more questions, reviewing the customers' current situation, and we just haven't uncovered their immediate pain point. Identify new prospects. Maybe you need to let the deals that's gone cold rest for a little while and then revisit them later. I've often found that after a cooling-off period, when I call on my old prospects again, it's met with a completely different attitude. In some situations, they're grateful to hear from you again. I've even found scenarios where they made another choice, and after a cooling off period, they realized they made a mistake and you come in and help them get back on the right track. They can turn into one of your most loyal customers. And finally, pray again. As James said, after praying again, the heavens gave rain and the earth bore fruit.

....

> Father, You are a great provider. You know the perfect time to answer all prayers. I know that You care, and I know that You hear my prayers, and from the moment I uttered the first word or thought the first thought, You heard my prayers, and they are answered "yes" and "amen"! Let my efforts bear fruit, Lord! In Jesus's name I pray. Amen!

DON'T GIVE UP

> Simon Peter said to them, "I am going fishing." They said to him, "We will go with you." They went out and got into the boat, but that night they caught nothing.
> —John 21:3

You ever wanted to give up or thought about going back to an old job or a change of professions? In today's verse that's exactly what Peter said he was going to do. His statement came shortly after the resurrection and prior to Jesus final ascension, Peter filled with what was discouragement, and I am sure still grieving, told the other disciples, "I am going fishing." This was not Peter just saying, "I am taking a personal day. I'm going out on the lake for a while," or "I'm hungry. I think I'll go see if the fish are biting." No, this was Peter saying, "I'm done with this. I'm going back to my old job of fishing." I know we have all felt that way at some point in our career. In our sales professions, the highs and lows can hit anyone emotionally. You're on top of the world one moment with a hard-fought victory, and you're at the lowest of lows with the next no from a customer. When those long seasons in between the next opportunity come along, it can be discouraging, defeating, and you may feel like Peter of just giving up and throwing in the towel. Suddenly, that old job where you used to work looks appealing. The other side of the fence seems so enticing. I find it interesting that with Peter's influence, the other disciples gave up as well and went with him. That's what happens sometimes; we get around others that feel like giving up, and it rubs off on us as well. But they were met with no success when they went back. It says they caught nothing that night. I've met so many sales reps over the years that changed job after job after job chasing easy sales. And every time they encountered a little difficulty, some turbulence, or a setback, they were ready to jump ship and move on. Sometimes even going back to a job, they left only to find those same old emotions were still there of why they left in the first place. Other times, they jump industries or professions only to be met with similar resistance. I have changed jobs several times myself, and I've changed industries multiple times as well. Sometimes for the right reasons, and sometimes probably like Peter, just out of discouragement and wanting what appears to be an easier life. I can say, every time I made a move without having clear guidance from the Lord, I was met with the same emotions, the same challenges, and the same temptation to bounce again. When we try to do it on our own and step outside of God's plan, chances are, we will have the same success that Peter and the disciples had and that is catching nothing.

John 21:4 says that the next morning, Jesus met them on the shore. When Jesus showed up, suddenly, the fish began to bite. It says they caught 153 large fish, and the net didn't even break. Now that's what I want in my life. I want the fish to bite. I want those customers to say yes, and those purchase orders to pour in. Jesus had a purpose for these disciples. He had a use for them, and it was not to just catch fish but to be fishing for people. Jesus had a purpose for their calling and for their lives. Perhaps that's you today. Maybe you're having those feelings: "This job is just too hard," "I need to quit," "I need to change jobs," or I should just go back to my old company. A famous college basketball coach once said, "Don't give up, don't ever give up." Sales friends, pray that God gives you clear guidance when it's time to move on otherwise stay put and wait for Jesus to show up. You, too, will have your sales nets filled.

> Father, You are the great provider. You know when we should stay and when we should go. I pray today that You will put people in my life that intend good and remove the ones that mean harm. Put the customers in my path that are ready to purchase. Give me wisdom on what to say, when to say it and the words to use. I thank You for all the blessings in my life. Amen.

GOD'S PROVISIONS

When they came to Capernaum, the collectors of the two-drachma tax went up to Peter and said, "Does your teacher not pay the tax?" He said, "Yes." And when he dame into the house, Jesus spoke to him first, saying "What do you think, Simon? From whom do kings of the earth take toll or tax? From their sons or from others?" And when he said, "From others," Jesus said to him "Then the sons are free. However, not to give offense to them, go to the sea and cast a hook and take the first fish that comes up, and when you open its mouth, you will find a shekel. Take and give it to them for me and for yourself."
—Matthew 17:24–27

God delights in providing. His creativity and the timeliness of His provisions are amazing. We see throughout the Bible examples of God's kindness and the unique way of when and how He decides to provide. From manna falling from the sky, bread, and meat by a raven; water from a rock; water into wine; endless supply of oil and flour in a jar; feeding thousands with a few fish and loaves of bread; an ark; and more. The Bible is filled with stories of God's continuous love and provisions for His people. He truly is Jehovah Jireh, provider of all.

In today's verses, Peter is asked by the tax collectors why Jesus hasn't paid His tax. So Jesus, using every opportunity to teach and coach His disciples on trusting and having faith, used this situation to provide in a unique way. He asks Peter to go catch a fish. Can you imagine Peter's amazement when he opens the fish's mouth, and there's a coin inside. Not only did Jesus provide enough to cover the tax, but a shekel was worth three times the value of a drachma. God wants to provide for you and bless you. It may come in the most unique way or at the most incredible time, but God will provide. I've often been focused on what I thought were my most important accounts only to have a customer seemingly appear from nowhere, make a purchase that helps me hit my quota for the month.

God's timing is perfect as well. When my wife and I decided to get married, I was new in my sales career. We were not completely broke, but we didn't have abundant funds as well. We decided on a simple wedding ceremony, a modest reception, but decided we would have a nice honeymoon, and she picked out a very nice wedding ring. It would be a real stretch to pay for all this. Wouldn't you know it, before we got married, I made a sizable sale. With that one sale, my commission was enough and almost to the penny that would cover the wedding, reception, our honeymoon, and the ring. Not only did God provide, but we won a free night in this beautiful bed-and-breakfast that we stayed in before we left for our honeymoon to Ireland. Every time we drive by that little B and B, we are reminded of how God uniquely provided for us at the very beginning of our marriage. I'm sure every time Peter saw a fish or was near that sea, he recalled God's unique provisions that day. Look over your customer list, think through some of those accounts that perhaps you haven't called on lately, then watch and see how God uniquely provides for you.

> Jesus, You are Jehovah Jireh. You are a great provider. I thank You for how You will uniquely provide for me today. Let me be careful to recognize Your hand in all that I do. I thank You and praise You today for Your provisions. In Jesus's name I pray. Amen.

REASON FOR OUR HOPE

But even if you should suffer for righteousness' sake, you will be blessed. Have no fear of them, nor be troubled, but in your hearts honor Christ the Lord as holy, always being prepared to make a defense to anyone who asks you for a reason for the hope that is in you; yet do it with gentleness and respect.
—1 Peter 3:14–15

We have all been around those individuals that just exhaust you with their attitudes. Every time you speak with them, they are just so worn out, grumbling, or complaining about something, underpaid, overworked, and they are always much busier than you can even imagine. Any time you ask them how they are doing, you'll always get this big sigh, and they'll just go on and on about how bad things are. If you are having a challenging day, they will one up you with a pitiful story of how bad they have it and let you know how much easier you have it over them. They can really drain your emotional battery if you let them. No doubt, you may find yourself wanting to avoid them. Customers are no different. If you are always complaining, moaning, and groaning, it is going to come across in your interactions with your clients and prospects. Although numerous considerations come into play on a purchase decision such as price, value, product quality, and performance, I think we would all agree, we would prefer to do business with people that we like. We like to be around individuals that are energetic, engaging, and filled with joy.

As Christians, we really should wear a different expression on our faces. The world should really be able to see joy and a spark in our life. Today's verses say we should always be prepared to let anyone know the reason for our hope. After all, as Christ followers we have the promise of eternal life. John 16:33 says, "I have told you these things, so that in me you may have peace. In this world you will have trouble. But take heart! I have overcome the world." That is our reason for hope. The Christian life is not one that promises to be easy, but it does promise that we are overcomers of the world. If we let our light shine through us, the people that we encounter daily will be intrigued as to what gives us hope. They will ask, "Where does this joy come from?" There's an old children's song that says, "This little light of mine, I'm going to let it shine." Let's let our light shine so that others may see the difference that resides within us.

....

> Jesus, You promise us eternal life. Let this promise shine through. Let my light shine. Let others see the hope and joy that comes from You. Thank You for all You do in our life! Amen!

WORK HEARTILY

> Whatever you do, work heartily, as for the Lord and not for men, knowing that from the Lord you will receive the inheritance as your reward. You are serving the Lord Christ.
> —Colossians 3:23–24

It takes twenty-one days to build a habit and ninety days to build a lifestyle. Prospecting can be one of the most challenging areas for any sales rep. It takes time, dedication, and continued perseverance and without seeing any results for months or years in some cases. It's hard, sometimes discouraging and challenging to dedicate yourself to this task. According to spotio, 40 percent of salespeople say prospecting is the most challenging part of the sales process. Statistics show that top producing sales reps will typically spend at least five hours a week on prospecting. Healthy habits take time to develop, and bad habits take even more time to break. If you are in a sales role that requires you to prospect for new clients, take time to spend cultivating new opportunities on a regular basis. It will pay huge dividends.

We also know that developing healthy spiritual habits can be hard, and it takes time as well. According to Pew Research, 67 percent of professing Christian men and 30 percent of women admit to rarely spending time in prayer. Reading the Bible doesn't fare well either; 41 percent say they never or seldom read their Bible according to a Gallup poll. Psalm 46:10 says, "Be still, and know that I am God. I will be exalted among the nations; I will be exalted in the earth!" Part of developing a good prayer life is getting alone with God. We need to slow down and be still with the Lord. Taking time to spend with God through His word and in prayer is a gift the Lord gave us to be able to communicate with Him. We just need to put the effort into develop this habit and make it a lifestyle. In sales and in our spiritual life we need to develop good healthy habits. We need to remember as Colossians 3:23–24 says we are to do our work for the Lord and not for men. We are to do our work heartily. This means to be enthusiastically and energetic. Good habits take time, but let us develop good spiritual habits by praying and reading God's word. It will pay huge dividends!

....

> Lord, You gave us Your word and prayer to speak to us every day if we will just spend that time. Help us to develop strong habits and healthy lifestyles. Give us the focus and determination to spend time in Your word and in prayer every day. Thank You, Father, for caring about our daily lives. We thank You for the inheritance we will receive through the precious blood of Jesus Christ! In His name, we pray! Amen.

MUSTARD-SEED FAITH

> He said to them, "Because of your little faith. For Truly, I say to you, if you have faith like a grain of mustard seed, you will say to this mountain, 'Move from here to there,' and it will move, and nothing will be impossible for you."
> —Matthew 17:20–21

The world mustard market is estimated to be around $9.9 billion. It takes over one thousand mustard seeds to make just one eight-ounce bottle of mustard. I can barely comprehend how many seeds that would take to meet the yearly demands for the mustard market. The Bible tells us if we have the faith of just one mustard seed, nothing is impossible for us. We can tell a mountain to move, and it will move. Now that is faith that I can barely comprehend as well.

The same can be said in our sales professions. I don't know how many times I hear salespeople talk about how terrible their company is, how poor their product performs, how expensive they are, how weak their territory is, how pathetic their customer list is, or how anemic are their leads. There's no way you can close deals with that mindset.

Matthew 17:16 says a boy's father brought his sick son to the disciples and they couldn't heal him. But Jesus rebuked the demon that was plaguing his son, and the boy was healed instantly. In the verses we read today in Matthew, Jesus is telling His disciples if they had only the faith of a grain of mustard seed, they could have healed this little boy as well. The key is not just having faith, but having faith in the one who heals. The secret in our sales roles is not having faith in our product, customers, or leads but in the one who can move those mountains and that is Jesus and Jesus alone. So take another look at those leads today, take a look at your customer list, take a look at what seems like a mountain in your life, and say, "In Jesus's name, mountain, move!

....

> Dear heavenly Father, we know that You can heal, and You can move mountains. We are asking You today to move mountains for us. Put the words in our mouth, put the customers on our minds, bring the prospects in our path, and help us move them. We know that nothing is impossible for You. We give You the praise. In Jesus's name we pray. Amen!

GO!

And Moses said to the people, "Fear not, stand firm, and see the salvation of the Lord, which he will work for you today. For the Egyptians whom you see today, you shall never see again. The Lord will fight for you, and you have only to be silent." The Lord said to Moses, "Why do you cry to me? Tell the people of Israel to go forward. Lift up your staff and stretch out your hand over the sea and divide it, that the people of Israel may go through the sea on dry ground.
—Exodus 14:13–16

When Moses was leading the people of Israel out of Egypt, they came to the banks of the Red Sea river with the enemy, Pharaoh's army bearing down on them. As they stood at the edge of the water, they started to be afraid and have doubts. They even questioned why Moses led them out of Egypt where they had been held captive and in bondage. But God was faithful throughout their journey. He had provided a pillar of clouds and fire to guide them, but as they faced the challenge of crossing over the river, they gave in to their fear. At the banks of the river is where God asks the question, "Why are you still crying out to me? Go!" When God has given you an answer, there comes a time for action. God was telling them, "I've got this, stop crying, and move out!"

I know a lot of salespeople that spend so much time prospecting, analyzing data, attending networking events, learning the products, overpreparing for meetings, planning to make calls, making a prospect list, entering information into a CRM, developing a spreadsheet; but they never get around to making the sales call, setting an appointment, meeting with the customer, or closing the deal. All the preliminary and premeeting activities are important, necessary, and vital; but if you never get around to talking to the customer, then you're not creating an opportunity or advancing the sale. Perhaps it's because of fear, maybe we have self-doubt, or we lack the confidence in our abilities, but there comes a time that the process requires action. There comes a point that just like God said to people of Israel, "It's go time." There's a general tendency for new salespeople to over-prepare and maybe even suffer from analysis paralysis, and they may struggle with having the confidence to execute and make the initial calls. They get stuck overthinking the process and never really generate the necessary outbound calls to start filling up their calendar with new clients. On the other hand, the more experienced rep will fail to put in the appropriate amount of time for meeting preparation or prospecting for new opportunities, often leaving their new sales funnel very dry. In both cases, action is required. God parted the Red Sea for the people of Israel, and they crossed on dry ground. When God tells us it's time to go, we will cross that sale river on dry ground as well.

I would suggest that if we have put in the time to prospect and prepare, then we need be people of action. We need to go and watch God part our Red Sea!

....

> Lord, You are a god of action. We come before You and ask You to part our Red Sea for us in our sales jobs. We give You the honor and the glory for all that You are doing! In Jesus's name. Amen.

TO ENTERTAIN OR NOT

For the kingdom of God is not a matter of eating and drinking but of righteousness and peace and joy in the Holy Spirit. Do not, for the sake of food, destroy the work of God. Everything is indeed clean, but it is wrong for anyone to make another stumble by what he eats. It is good not to eat meat or drink wine or do anything that causes your brother to stumble.
—Romans 14:17, 20–21

One of the dilemmas that an outside sales rep must face is with the question of entertaining clients. What is acceptable, and when should you use restraint? If you work in an industry or for a company where entertaining customers is a requirement or part of the culture, it can sometimes be a real challenge on how you balance your personal, family, and work life. Not to mention, the conflict that can arise when you are striving to make choices using your Christian moral compass as your guide. You can easily feel compelled to compromise your standards, feel obligated, or even pressured to join in with the crowd.

It never ceases to amaze me that some of the choices reps will make when it's under the guise of showing a customer a good time. I have seen reps lose their jobs because they overindulged and made inappropriate comments. I recently witnessed a rep at a customer appreciation event no less, get inebriated, insult their customer, and lose that account all because of a poor choice. Too many times, individuals will cross moral boundaries all in the name of entertainment. There is nothing inherently wrong with having fun, laughing, eating, and enjoying being with your customers or coworkers. Ecclesiastes 3 even says there is a time to laugh and a time to dance. After all, there are numerous examples of Jesus showing warm hospitality to others. He turned water into wine at a wedding ceremony. He visited friends in their homes. He fed thousands. He cooked breakfast for his disciples, dined with them, and even went fishing with them. Jesus even told Timothy to drink a little wine for his stomach issues.

If being social and enjoying the company of people is okay, then when does it become wrong or cross over the line? First Peter 4:8 says we should be sober-minded. This means we should keep a clear head and make good choices. The verses that we read today in Romans 14 tell us there are things that we can do and may be permissible, but if doing certain actions causes another person to stumble, we should reconsider or refrain from those activities. Ephesians 5 gives us the right course of action. It tells us to be filled with the spirit, walk as children of the light, and take no part in the unfruitful works of darkness. The Bible has plenty of examples for moderation. It tells us to be reasonable, not to use our freedom as an opportunity for the flesh, be a role model of good works, have integrity, be reverent, and be dignified. My sales rep friends, if we are followers of Christ, we have been set apart, we are a new creation, and we are children of the light. Let us be filled with the spirit.

....

> Lord, thank You for creating us to enjoy laughter, to enjoy fun, food, and fellowship of others. We know that You tell us to be children of light and moderation. We ask for Your guidance when we're entertaining customers and let us always be prepared to tell them of our hope that we have! In Jesus's name I pray! Amen.

NEVER STOP LEARNING

An intelligent heart acquires knowledge, and
the ear of the wise seeks knowledge.
—Proverbs 18:15

Henry Ford, the famous automaker, once said, "Anyone who stops learning is old, whether at twenty or eighty. Anyone who keeps learning stays young." As professional sales representatives, we must always continue to grow and learn. Chip Ingram, in the book *Good to Great in God's Eyes*, makes a few suggestions, as Christians, we should think great thoughts, read great books, pursue great people, and develop great habits.

As a professional sales rep, we should never reach a point where we stop pursuing knowledge. Stay up to date, fresh, and current on trends, products, and new techniques. Continually read books, trade journals, and industry publications. Take courses that will keep your skillset current. Attend seminars, webinars, and listen to podcasts that challenge your thinking. Watch educational shows on a new topic or idea. Explore new subjects. Attend tradeshows, workshops, and conferences even one's that are not completely related to your company. Observe high-performing sales reps even if they're in a completely different vertical market or industry than yours. Collaborate and network with industry leaders and thought leaders.

Albert Einstein said, "The important thing is not to stop questioning; curiosity has its own reason for existing." Never lose your curiosity to learn new things and take an interest in new ideas and meet new people. Let's strive to not be the type of person that thinks they know everything. The same person that is always telling others about the way we used to do things. There's nothing wrong with experience and historical reference, but we should always strive to gain more information and knowledge. "The beautiful thing about learning is nobody can take it away from you," B. B. King once said. Let us never get complacent with the skills, gifts, and talents that God has given to us.

....

> My Savior and Lord, thank You for giving me the ability to learn. Let me never take for granted the special talents You have given me. Thank You for blessing me in my work, with my family, and in my endeavors. Thank You, Jesus! Amen!

GRATITUDE IS CONTAGIOUS

> The Lord bless you and keep you; the Lord make his face to shine upon you and be gracious to you; the Lord lift up his countenance upon you and give you peace.
> —Numbers 6:24–25

How important is gratitude to being a successful salesperson?

I recently read an article that quoted a *Harvard Business Review Study* that said you're *37 percent better at sales* when you have an attitude of gratitude. Having an attitude of gratitude is especially true with our customers. Saying thank you costs us nothing but being non-appreciative can carry a brutally high cost. I read another study that says it costs five times as much to attract a new customer than keeping an existing one: 50 percent of existing satisfied customers are willing to try a new product, and they are willing to spend 31 percent more.

I had a recent experience where I was the customer at a retail tire shop where I was being made to feel like I was a complete inconvenience to the rep even though I had just bought the higher-priced set of tires from them. I started to light him up and remind him that I was the customer. After rethinking my strategy, I decided to show him some gratitude instead. I said, "Thank you for servicing my vehicle," "Thank you for scheduling my appointment," and "Thank you for taking care of my vehicle." His reaction was an immediate about-face, like I had given him a happy pill or something. It is amazing how someone will respond to a simple kind word, gesture, or a simple thank-you!

Showing gratitude and appreciation costs us nothing but can have long-lasting future benefits. One customer experience agency found that loyal customers are five times as likely to forgive, five times as likely to repurchase, seven times as likely to try a new offering, and four times as likely to make a referral.

So let's make every attempt to be more appreciative of every penny *anyone* buys from us! Trust me, I am the king of being sandpaper to an arrogant or unappreciative customer, but I challenge each of us to show more gratitude for our business and see if it helps! If you haven't told your best customers "Thanks" in a while—make sure you do—they will greatly appreciate it!

....

> Father, help me to have a grateful heart. Let me always show my appreciation with my customers, coworkers, friends, and family. Thank You for all that You do in my life. I am grateful that I am a child of Yours. In Jesus's name. Amen!

ABOUT THE AUTHOR

Tim Carroll is a top-performing sales professional, coach, mentor, and leader. He has a diverse business background in sales, leadership, and management having worked across various industries and vertical markets. With over twenty years of sales experience, his client list includes numerous Global and Fortune 500 companies. He previously owned a sales representative agency focused on the automotive and marine markets and held positions as a frontline sales hunter for several companies. He has served as the vice president of sales for a regional technology integrator, territory sales manager for a privately held global technology manufacturer, and currently serves as the mid-Atlantic sales manager for a multibillion-dollar technology and electronics manufacturer. Tim is keenly aware of the sales strategies required to produce results across multiple industries and today's complexities of incorporating your Christian faith in the sales environment.

He graduated from the University of North Texas and served in the United States Air Force as an aerospace physiologist. He has served as a deacon, led the marriage ministry at his former church, coached youth sports, been a guest college lecturer and a small group teacher. Tim was a founding board member for the Lake Norman IT Professionals, member of the Lake Norman Economic Development Group, and served on the board for Voice Box Ministries. He has a passion for leadership, the study of great leaders, and incorporating his faith into the business community.

Tim Carroll currently resides in Cornelius, North Carolina, with his wife Carla and their two sons, Clayton and Caleb.

Printed in the USA
CPSIA information can be obtained
at www.ICGtesting.com
LVHW041157221124
797246LV00001B/21